Praise for Monique G...

#1 E... ...woman's

"Greenwood knows a thing or two about having it all." —*Newsday*

"Monique Greenwood has given sisters a gift that's right on time and right on target. Filled with her wisdom, humor, and love, *Having What Matters* is an invitation to create the meaningful life we all want and deserve." —Susan L. Taylor, editorial director, *Essence*

"*Having What Matters* is a must. Monique covers everything that matters in a way that truly does. It's everything so many books claim to be—for real." —Dr. Bertice Berry, motivational speaker and author of *Redemption Song* and *The Haunting of Hip-Hop*

"Sistahs will revel in this guide that finally teaches us how to look great, manage finances, and more, all with balance and grace." —Terrie M. Williams, celebrity publicist and author of *Personal Touch* and *Stay Strong*

"If you've been looking for a place to go for help on how to change from your superwoman garb to a way of life that not only fits you better but tickles your heart, then, my sisters, go immediately between the covers of Monique Greenwood's *Having What Matters*." —Johnetta B. Cole, author of *Dream the Boldest Dreams* and president emerita of Spelman College

"In this book and in her life, Monique Greenwood illustrates perfectly how we all can have professional success and self-satisfaction." —Dr. Suzan Johnson Cook, pastor, author of *Sister Strength,* and president of the New York Coalition of 100 Black Women

"A pioneer . . . Greenwood has made herself into a mini-mogul." —*Crain's New York Business*

"The superwoman offers feel-good advice for 'sistahs.' Readers will feel compelled to listen to her; after all, she started at 'ground zero' and worked her way up to the top."

—*Publishers Weekly*

Successful entrepreneur, bestselling author, and acclaimed motivational speaker MONIQUE GREENWOOD is the owner of Akwaaba Enterprises, Inc., a lifestyle and hospitality company, which includes Brooklyn, New York–based Akwaaba Mansion Bed and Breakfast, Akwaaba Café, Mirrors Coffee House, and Akwaaba Properties, a real estate holding company. Her latest venture is Akwaaba by the Sea, a bed-and-breakfast in Cape May, New Jersey, the country's oldest seaside resort.

A twenty-year communications veteran, Ms. Greenwood most recently served as editor-in-chief of *Essence* magazine and is the co-author of *The Go On, Girl! Book Club Guide to Reading Groups*.

She lives in Brooklyn with her husband of thirteen years (who still calls her "love goddess") and her ten-year-old daughter (who calls her "cool").

An Imprint of HarperCollins*Publishers*

HAVING
WHAT
MATTERS

*The Black Woman's Guide to
Creating the Life You Really Want*

Monique Greenwood

A hardcover edition of this book was published in 2001 by William Morrow, an imprint of HarperCollins Publishers.

HarperCollins books may be purchased for educational, business, or sales promotional use. For information, please write: Special Markets Department, HarperCollins Publishers Inc., 10 East 53rd Street, New York, NY 10022.

FIRST AMISTAD PAPERBACK EDITION 2002

Designed by Gretchen Achilles

Printed on acid-free paper

The Library of Congress has catalogued the hardcover edition as follows:

Greenwood, Monique.
    Having what matters / Monique Greenwood.—1st ed.
      p. cm.
   ISBN 0-688-17509-0
   1. African American women—Life skills guides.   2. Success—United States—Handbooks, manuals, etc.   3. Professional employees—United States—Life skills guides.   I. Title.

E185.86 .G74   2001
646.7'0082—dc21   2001016684

  ISBN 0-06-050788-8 (pbk.)

02   03   04   05   06   QW   10 9 8 7 6 5 4 3 2 1

To Glenn and Glynn,
may you always know how much you matter

CONTENTS

Acknowledgments

Endless gratitude and love to my parents, Joann and Carl Greenwood, whose unshakable belief in me taught me to believe in myself and in my God. And to my mother-in-law, Mary Frances Pogue, who wrapped her arms around me twelve years ago and never let go.

Much respect and honor to my grandmother, Virginia Lemons, whose youthful attitude and appearance at age 93 inspires me; and to my dearly departed grandfather, Benjamin Greenwood, whose entrepreneurial spirit ignites me.

A lifetime of devotion to my siblings, Vaughn, Ronald, Donald, and Gina, and their mates, Kim, Taunya, and Rodger. I couldn't have asked for more lovable—and likable—brothers and sisters if the choice were mine.

Smooches to my always supportive sister circle: Ieola Bakr, Crystal Bobb-Semple, Tracy Mitchell-Brown, Karen Brydie, Jacqueline Contee, Lynda Johnson, Benilde Little, Jacqui Williams-Foy, Benita Wynn, and the Go On Girls!

A jeweled crown to my mentor Susan L. Taylor, whose grace and strength serve as a shining example of black womanhood for me and for so many others.

Heartfelt appreciation to the Akwaaba family. Your dedication and commitment are crucial to my vision of community empowerment. We can do it!

A big shout-out to my Bedford-Stuyvesant community, a place with beautiful brownstones and even more beautiful brown people.

Finally, when it comes to this book, it would not have been possible without the patience and priceless love of my husband, Glenn, and daughter, Glynn; the "get-real" intervention of my friend Sandra Dorsey Rice; the pep talks and gentle prodding of my agent, Victoria Sanders; the faith and guidance of the pros at HarperCollins Publishers; and the brilliance and generosity of my dear Essence friends: Michelle Burford, Donina Burke, Patrik Henry Bass, Joy Duckett Cain, Rosemarie Robotham, LaVon Leak-Wilks, and especially Ylonda Gault Caviness.

HAVING
WHAT
MATTERS

INTRODUCTION

I live in an eighteen-room mansion, have a closet filled with designer clothes and shoes, own four prosperous businesses—two bed-and-breakfast inns, a restaurant, and a coffeehouse—and I've served as editor-in-chief of *Essence,* the preeminent magazine for black women. Because I was starting from ground zero, I knew it wouldn't be easy to check off each of my childhood dreams, but I knew it was possible. I, like so many black women, have inherited a crown passed down from millions of nameless, faceless, "ansisters" whose sacrifice and struggle, faith and fortitude, have made it possible for sisters today to soar.

As recently as the hedonistic eighties, an accumulation of things and titles would have been enough to proclaim one successful. But in this new millennium it's no longer about "she who has the most toys wins." The new mantra is "she who has the most joy wins!" No longer are we obsessed with "having it all," but we do want to have "what matters." We may not want that corner office and big paycheck, for example, if it means we're constantly stressed out and can't remember the last time we had a date with our man—that's if we've even made time to attract one.

I'm not going to pretend otherwise—living in a mansion is grand. But what really makes it heavenly is not the number of rooms but the fact that I've turned my home into a haven where I replenish my soul. Those designer clothes? They adorn a non-model-size body I have grown to love; that, my sister, is priceless. My businesses? They are part of my life mission, which is to help empower my people. That's what really matters to me. Even higher on my list of what matters is that my neighbors call me friendly, my friends call me loyal, my nine-year-old daughter calls me cool, my husband of twelve years still calls me love goddess, and I call myself a child of God.

I firmly believe that success is personal fulfillment and satis-faction. There is no one-size-fits-all definition, because success is so subjective. Or at least it should be. What rocks my world may feel like a rock in your shoe, but I do believe there are some com-mon desires we all have—money in the bank, a fit body and fabu-lous style, a loving circle of friends and family, a way to leave the world a better place, and just plain ol' peace of mind.

And guess what? I believe we can all have those things! For as long as I can remember, I've believed this, even though I wasn't born to the manor, not even to a room of my own. As a struggling college student still living at home and sleeping in the same dou-ble bed I shared with my high-school sister, I could see myself successful and enjoying life's riches. I had a lot of nerve envision-ing such, huh? After all, there was no trust fund waiting for me to come of age, no last name that opened doors, no private-school diploma or Ivy League degree, no drop-dead-gorgeous Naomi Campbell face or bod.

What I did have was a desire to be a winner and a willingness to work diligently to come from behind and end up out front. In short, what I had back then and still have now is what Floyd Flake, the former congressman and prominent pastor of New York's Allen AME Church, calls a "bootstrapper" mentality. That is, the mind-set that I am not a victim but a person with the power to ride out and rise above the pain and difficulty of the moment, knowing without a doubt that joy and peace would be mine. If obstacles present themselves, I step around them. If opportunities don't present themselves, I create them.

If you have the same mentality, and I suspect you do, this book is for you. I wrote it for sisters of all ages to first encourage us to define success for ourselves. Not the success our girlfriend has. Not the success Mama says we should have. But the inner and outer success that would make *you* want to shout, "It's a beautiful life!" from the highest mountaintop. Then *Having What Matters* acknowledges some universal goals we all strive for—a great career, financial freedom, a sexy soul mate, a stylish look and healthy body, loving family and friends, time for self, a way to make the world better—and offers a practical, step-by-step blueprint for achieving them. My very own life—from anonymity to the top of the *Essence* masthead, from an unfit size-eighteen body to a shapely size twelve, from a cramped rental apartment to a mansion of my own, from countless bad relationships to a sweet union—is evidence that it works.

Now, this is not the kind of book you merely read—you must *do*. I know how some of us sisters "watch" Billy Blanks do tae-bo on TV as if that's enough to get rid of our unwanted pounds. But when you read the "Financial Freedom" chapter in this book, for example, you must make a spending plan. And when you read the "Sexy Soul Mate" chapter, you might want to go ahead and pull out that red dress! Remember that bootstrappers are doers, and *doing* is the underlying principle of this book. I know that you may be feeling you can't "do" another thing. Most of us are truly overworked and overwhelmed. But it's not about adding to your to-do list. It's about taking time to reflect so that you focus your time and energy on doing "what matters."

When a book editor called me about this project, I couldn't imagine how I would add another thing to my already arm-length list of obligations. In fact, after I said yes to the book, I called my agent crying and told her I had changed my mind. I just couldn't see how I would find the time to write it. But after I made the decision to call the project off, I had fitful sleep for a week. I came to realize that writing this book really did matter to me. While I am not a celebrity, a success coach, or a spiritual guru—just an ordinary sister trying to live an extraordinary life—I have met far too many women who marveled at my life and somehow didn't understand that they could create a life of their own that would be just as impressive. I felt the burning need to show them how.

So I took a page from my unwritten book and followed my own advice for getting things done. I remembered that the number-one question people ask me is "How do you do it all?" My answer has always been "I don't do it all. I do what matters." I explain that I've learned to say no to those things I'm not passionate about, and I've minimized time spent with people who drain me. I've surrounded myself with individuals who believe in me and support my efforts, and I've made time to nurture and rejuvenate myself so that I can go back out and do the critical work I'm convinced I was born to do. With that in mind, I took a leave of absence from two community boards I'm active on, hired a director of operations to keep a close eye on my restaurant and coffeehouse, and went away for a restorative week at the beach before tackling an outline for the book. You are now holding in your hands the results of that effort, something I hope will matter to you greatly.

Chapter 1

A LEGACY OF GREATNESS

*Y*ou and I, my sister, are the children of the dream. Our ability to secure decent, and in some cases top-paying jobs is the result of the blood, sweat, and tears of our parents, our grandparents, and our enslaved ancestors before them. It is through their lives that we can learn principle and pride. Of course, the struggle is not over and the road is not unfettered. But the fact is, we have gone from picking cotton to picking blue-chip stocks. It humbles me to be able to move ahead because of the sacrifices made by those who came before me.

Success is our birthright, given the monumental challenges we have fought to overcome. Some of our struggles have made the history books and some have not. I need look no further than my own family tree to see how the indomitable spirit and determination of our people have won out over hardships and obstacles.

In the early 1920s my grandfather Benjamin Ordway Greenwood opened a modest corner grocery store in southeast Washington, D.C. But a white man with a competing store across the street complained to the wholesaler that he didn't want his food delivered in the same truck as a black man's. The wholesaler caved in and stopped delivery of my grandfather's goods.

Papa, as we called him, didn't grow bitter, just more determined. He scraped together enough money to buy a horse and wagon, then picked up the groceries himself from the wholesaler's warehouse. When Papa wasn't carrying food to his store, he hauled trash for other businesses. In the process a moving business was born—Greenwood's Transfer Moving and Storage Company. It would go on to become one of the country's leading black-owned businesses.

In 1927 Papa bought his first truck and expanded his business to include transporting horses, which at that time were still used to pull wagons. When automobiles took over the roadways, that end of the business came to a halt. But my grandfather changed with the times. He knew that the only way to make the family business grow was to secure federal contracts. That would mean financing, since the government took about a month to pay its bills. Papa knocked on door after door until one bank, National Capital, granted a line of credit to a hardworking black man who always paid his bills on time.

As inspiring a story as Papa's is, you might think I grew up hearing it. Hardly. In fact, in the early eighties, had I not found myself rummaging through a drawer of report cards and other documents looking for my college degree, I might never have learned of Papa's struggles at all. In my search I came across a yellowed newspaper article from the front page of a 1975 edition of the *Washington Post*. "Oldest D.C. Black-Owned Firm Grew with Effort," the headline read. And there, under the big type, was a small photo of my grandfather in his cap and knickers, standing in front of the truck he bought in 1927. The article detailed the growth of Papa's business and the fortitude of a man with vision. It said that in 1983, Greenwood's Transfer Moving and Storage Company made *Black Enterprise* magazine's list of the nation's top one hundred black businesses, boasting gross sales of $1.5 million!

I screamed! I had no idea that the family business my daddy had worked for as a moving man all my life was so successful, no idea of my grandfather's amazing fortitude. My Aunt Helen took over the business in 1964 when Papa died. I was only five. My father sold my aunt his share of the stock Papa had left him to help pay down the mortgage on the house he and my mother raised us five kids in (they still live there today). So my father had a moving man's salary, and I had no idea of the company's greatness.

I ran through the house clutching that newspaper, looking for my father, looking for an explanation. "Why didn't you tell me about Papa—all he went through, all he accomplished?" I demanded when I met up with my daddy. My father at first looked puzzled. Then he took a deep breath and explained. Papa's success had been tinged with the shame of having doors closed in his face, tainted by the reality of black entrepreneurs simply not having the same options as whites. Papa, my father told me, had wanted to shield his family from the pain and humiliation of his being treated as less than a man because of the color of his skin. And although he was proud of the moving business, he might never have started it at all had that wholesaler decided not to deliver a black man's groceries.

But what Papa regarded as a shameful chapter, I saw as testament to a true bootstrapper's will and commitment. Papa showed the world that while discrimination might slow him down, nothing could stop him from pressing on. And even though I came to know that part of my history relatively late in life, it has ignited in me a burning determination as well.

The Bootstrapper's Way

Papa's story is a clear example of a poor, black man in America bootstrapping his way to the top. A bootstrapper is a person of very modest means who, by dint of sheer will and determination, excels beyond imagination. A bootstrapper doesn't have much, but a bootstrapper doesn't need much either. Through my Papa, and perhaps your mama or papa, there is a powerful lesson in creating your own destiny—even if you're one generation, or one paycheck, away from poverty. A bootstrapper casts her bucket where she is and begins to run the race with fortitude and conviction. Like the old Nike ad slogan, she can "Just Do It" because she believes that she can. Sure, she seizes opportunity, but she also stands at the ready to *make* opportunity.

Some people regard the term "bootstrapper" as a loaded one, full of ultraconservative undertones. In some circles it harks back to the political-speak of the establishment who maintain that all us black folks need to do to excel is "pull ourselves up by our bootstraps" and work hard "like European immigrants and others have done." This model completely ignores the unique place African-Americans have in a society that, despite its progress, is fundamentally racist and sexist.

That's not the kind of bootstrapping I'm talking about. Rather than *ignore* the fact that struggle is a very real and distinct element of the black experience, my view of a bootstrapper embraces it. For us, bootstrapping demands that we draw upon that struggle, tapping in to our innate ability as "children of the dream" to succeed in the face of great odds.

My definition of a bootstrapper runs deeper than superficial material accomplishments. While wealth building is certainly a tenet of success, it is almost a side effect. To my mind, the bootstrapper concept also has much to do with drive and inner striving. For example, you will never hear a bootstrapping sister make these kinds of statements:

+ "It's not good for a sister to be too smart or too successful; no brother will want you."

+ "Why should I break my back working hard? I've got a job. I do *all right*."

+ "Life's a bitch: You work, you pay taxes, then you die."

+ "Since I don't have a college degree, computer skills, or [fill in the blank], I can't achieve my dreams."

+ "The white man is going to allow me to get only so far. So there's no sense trying."

No, a bootstrapper knows better. Like our hardworking ansisters, a bootstrapper lives from a deep knowing within her being. She knows that her determination can take her anywhere she wants to go. And when she wakes up in the morning and looks in the mirror—even on those days when her hair is matted and her face swells from lack of sleep—she can look into her own eyes and say out loud, "The world is mine."

Bootstrapping strikes a chord in the heart and soul of who we are as black folk. You see, a bootstrapper comes by her striver's mentality honestly. She got it from her people, who got it from theirs. She doesn't have, nor does she need, the usual entrées to success, like high-powered connections. Is a bootstrapper smarter than the rest of us? Yes and no.

Bootstrappers are definitely intelligent. But what's more important is that they have a keen mother wit, which—in case your mother never told you—is separate and apart from book learning and more sophisticated than plain street smarts. A bootstrapper has the innate ability to size up her circumstances quickly, accurately. Because in the end it matters little that a situation is fair or equitable; only that it *is*. This is not to say that a bootstrapper does not have ideals. Quite the contrary. But rather than muse upon the idyllic nature of how things should be, she tries to find a pragmatic way to make her ideals a reality.

This pragmatism is almost second nature to a bootstrapper. By instinctively developing strategies with which to navigate the landscape, a bootstrapper simply *makes* things happen. She finds a way when there appears to be no way. Give a bootstrapper lemons and she will not stop at making lemonade. She will dream of becoming the Starbucks of lemonade and eventually turn her citrus concoction into a thriving retail chain, e-commerce site, wholesale and import/export empire. See, it's when by all appearances a bootstrapper has been beaten down that she rises like a phoenix and takes flight.

Magic? Hardly. Bootstrappers are some of the hardest-working folk on the face of the planet. We're like little elves—get up early and stay up late, work while others are sleeping. We're working while others are partying, shopping, or gossiping. Those on the outside can rarely see it or identify with it. They look at us as though God's bounties simply fall into our laps. Perhaps that's because we don't talk about it much. It's not that we don't get tired or frustrated. We just don't sit around complaining about it. Primarily because we're too busy. But it's also because we know we're blessed, and we see all the work we're doing as part of our purpose.

Your background may not be a mirror reflection of my own, and you may not have faced the same struggles. Like me, you, too, are wholly and categorically unique. But bootstrappers do share a certain set of values and a way of looking at the world. We use the bootstrapper approach in every area of our lives. It influences our careers, our personal goals, our relationships with family and friends—even our inner dialogues with ourselves.

How about you? Do you "see" yourself living out your dreams? And do these dreams happen to include things like these:

+ Loving a good brother and being loved in return?

+ Looking hot and feeling good?

+ Getting the most out of your career?

+ Having enough bank to enjoy life's finer things *and* have financial security?

+ Feeling spiritually connected and motivated to leave the world a better place?

Okay. We may be onto something here. But here's the next step. It's one thing to *want* many of the same things as a bootstrapper. It's quite another to actually *be* a bootstrapper. To see if you're one, consider the following:

1. You're a "real" sister. You don't front or put on airs. You can flow among professional women and around-the-way girls with the greatest of ease and enjoy the company of each.

2. You can delay gratification. As a kid, you were probably one of those for whom the candy Now and Later truly meant eat some now and save the rest of the package for later. Now that you're grown, you still have no trouble putting off short-term pleasures for long-term gains.

3. You're a worker bee. You will do whatever it takes to get a job done—grunt work and all. In fact, you'll sometimes work so hard you let yourself go.

4. You're resilient. When things don't go your way, you try again, because you know that success does not make you and fail-

ure does not break you. You learn from your mistakes and press on.

5. You're wise, which is not the same as being smart. You assess a situation based not only upon what is visible but upon those things unseen and left unspoken. You've been told that you have a sort of "sixth sense."

6. You're a people person. You were popular in school, and to this day people seem to be drawn to you. "Pretentious" is not a word most people would use to describe you.

7. You do several tasks at once. You simply hate to waste time, so you squeeze something productive out of most every moment. You're reading while you're eating and working while you ride the train.

8. You are fiercely independent. Even those you love hold little sway once you make a decision from the heart. You define your life's goals and aspirations on your own terms.

9. You honestly feel you *deserve* to be well off. You have no intention of settling for a humdrum, middling lifestyle. You believe that prosperity is yours; you are worthy of enjoying all God's riches.

10. You're generous. You know that what you put out, you get back manifold. Besides, you genuinely enjoy helping others realize their goals. So no matter how busy you are, you *always* have time to give another sister or brother advice or share information.

11. You're competitive, but mostly with yourself. You're aware of the achievements of those around you, and they spur you to push ahead. You're constantly trying to outdo yourself—top last year's achievement.

12. You enjoy being a black woman. Sure, you have days when you're less than thrilled with the face and bod looking back at you in the mirror. But by and large you think you've got it going on. And without being a hootch about it, you like to strut your stuff—happy hips and all!

13. You're not necessarily "supposed" to make it. Perhaps no one else in your family went to college or excelled professionally. You may have even been told somewhere along the way that you "want too much" or "work too hard," because the fact is that few people expect you to succeed in the face of the odds.

14. Family matters to you. Whether you have a husband and kids or not and even if your parents are no longer living, your values are rooted in a strong sense of connection to a loving circle of folks for whom you care deeply.

If you saw yourself in most of the above, we're kindred spirits. The truth is, most of us black women have the makings of a bootstrapper. All some of us need is a little coaching and some prodding to tap that bootstrapper within and let her take center stage in our lives.

Think of the next several chapters as an adventure. Not only am I going to take you for a ride, I'm going to be cruising shotgun right alongside. All us bootstrappers—both veterans and neophytes—need to sharpen our attitudes from time to time.

More so than a success vehicle or some sort of complex formula, bootstrapping is all about attitude. It's both the means and the end, the journey and the destination. You will learn that the bootstrapper inside you is also your fighting mechanism. I can tell you from my own experience that it is the inner strength and motivation and personal power—all mixed with God's grace—that allows me to stare down adversity and forge ahead with determination.

I'll give you an example. Just months after the announcement of my appointment as *Essence* editor-in-chief, the major media were beating a path to my door. On one of the very first interviews I granted, the reporter spent several hours interviewing me. And, like any good journalist, she spoke with the people on my staff to gauge their reactions to the news. One young sister-editor anonymously voiced her skepticism, questioning whether I would be able to juggle my many roles as an entrepreneur with the demands of running a magazine. Naturally, I was dismayed to find out that there was a dissenter among the ranks, and my first instinct was to confront the source immediately when I discovered who it was.

But when I looked closer at the situation, I realized that after all that time the reporter had spent talking to me, she still missed the "essence" of Monique Greenwood. So did the sister who tried to put me down.

The fact is, my heart beats with that of other black women. My outside endeavors were hardly a distraction. If anything, my business enterprises brought me closer to the *Essence* reader, closer to the *Essence* mission. At the bed-and-breakfast, the restaurant, and the coffeehouse, I have intimate contact with sisters. I have come to realize that those words that were meant to impugn my mandate were actually a blessing, because they presented me an opportunity—to prove them wrong.

When I was the subject of another media profile, again the reporter was sharp and had obviously done her homework. She alluded to the newspaper article and asked outright for my response to the critic who speculated that I couldn't possibly handle all that I do. My response was simple and to the point. "A lot of people will try to water you down," I said. "But I'm like concentrate. When you pour water on me, I just get bigger."

Great sound bite, right? But I truly believe it. If you are ever to accomplish your goals, you, too, must filter out the comments, criticisms, and admonishments of others.

Besides, for reasons I've never completely understood, it is very difficult for some people to be happy about the success of others. The way I see it, there is such abundance in the universe that there's more than enough prosperity for all of us. Some people will just resent the fact that you *want* to get ahead. You reflect for them the uncomfortable fact that they're not happy with their status quo but doing very little to change it. Do your own thing anyway.

A Child's Eye

I know now as an adult just how blessed I was to have two loving parents who continually affirmed me. As youngsters, my siblings and I had our each and every accomplishment lauded to the hilt. If I drew a picture or wrote an essay in school, over and over again I heard words like "This is the prettiest picture I've ever seen!" or "You're such a smart girl!"

The message was clear and resounding: Monique, you are special. I grew up believing it with every fiber of my being. So when I dreamed of various career choices, aspirations, and life goals, the question in my mind was never "if," but always "how." There was no doubt that I had the power within me to reach the highest heights possible. Nothing was beyond reach.

Of course, as a young girl I assumed that everyone had parents like mine, that everyone knew their "specialness." Boy, was I wrong. Many sisters are like battle-weary war veterans—walking around bearing the open wounds of deeply troubled childhoods. Sadly, for some that means outright physical or mental abuse. There are others who suffer from issues of abandonment or betrayal, where one or both parents deserted the family, either by choice or by force. Most often, though, childhood scars are the result of much subtler injuries. Many parents were just so busy trying to put food on the table, they failed to give their children time and emotional attention. Some women were brought up in that old-school mind-set, where children were to be seen but not heard. They were not granted the opportunity to have their dreams and goals validated.

Most of these parents, of course, didn't mean their children any harm. More than likely they were not nurtured as children themselves. You can't be mad at them for doing what they believed was right.

Affirm Thyself

It's easy to bemoan the lack of attention or material things you didn't get as a child. And its even easier still to make excuses for yourself based on some injustice—real or imagined—you were forced to endure as a little girl. But the fact of the matter is, what's done is done. While you cannot go back in time and undo the suffering, you can do something today to start the healing. Too many of us sit around giving too much of our energy away to the past. That is not the bootstrapper's way. The classic bootstrapper adopts the wise words of spiritual teacher Deepak Chopra, who once said, "The past is history. The future is not promised. Right now is a gift. That's why it is called the present."

Starting right here and right now, you *can* shift your thinking, even if it's the same mind-set you have carried with you throughout your entire life. What your parents or your childhood did not give you, you can give yourself. The way to start is by remapping your state of consciousness.

If you did not grow up surrounded by parents who championed your every good deed, it's not too late to become your own cheering section. Many of us, myself included, have been conditioned to look for approval from the outside. And while I think it's great to have grown up in a home rich with affirmation, even I have had to come to grips with the reality that not everyone is rooting for me. I realized long ago that the encouragement and faith I needed to achieve my goals had to come from me. I pat myself on the back all the time, even when I'm not doing so well.

If any of this strikes a chord, then you've been doing your inner work like a bootstrapping sister-girl should. Part of being a bootstrapper is committing yourself to a sort of inner discovery. By definition, a bootstrapper is self-aware. She knows her inner failings but shuns the futile cycle of denial and blame games. Instead, she works on where she is right now and determines from that how to get to where she wants to be. Are you:

+ Capable of a lot more than you're doing?

+ Frustrated by your station in life?

+ Bored with your life?

+ Stuck in your comfort zone—unwilling to take a big risk that will likely catapult you to where you want to be?

What's stopping you from getting further in life? Don't just shrug your shoulders. Think about this honestly. And if the answers displease you, don't think you are alone. Every day many of us put our happiness on layaway. We think we're going to come back and somehow claim it later—after we lose weight, after we get a new job, after we kick a brother to the curb, after we find a new brother to replace him. The list goes on and on. Don't wait any longer to seize your good. The "perfect" time and season will never come. There is no better time than right now to begin pointing your life in a new direction. If you don't know where to start, how about trying my "P-soup" recipe for success. You will need:

+ Planning and Preparation

+ Persistence and Patience

+ Passion and Purpose

+ Positive role models and Patting yourself on the back

As you can see, the ingredients are basic and wholesome—you're bound to have them lying around somewhere; it's just a matter of whipping them up. The formula is simple—you'll have to use plenty of old-fashioned elbow grease to knead the mixture, but it's nothing you can't handle. And best of all, the results are foolproof. This recipe yields guaranteed results. It may not turn out as you imagined, but your efforts are sure to give rise to an absolutely delectable creation.

Planning and Preparation

We all have goals. There is probably not a sister among us who doesn't dream of taking the world by storm and setting it off. But how many of us know those sisters (or brothers, for that matter) who seem to always talk up a field of dreams? They have a critical case of the "I'm gonna's"—as in "I'm gonna start my own business" or "I'm gonna go back to school."

These folks are not liars. They have every honorable desire to change the course of their lives. But what they're missing is a *plan*—a strategy that will turn that dream into a reality. Planning is the one critical, but often overlooked, step on the journey toward change. And it's no wonder. A plan can seem daunting. It requires that we, for a brief time anyway, get still, something that few of us are quick to do. It means putting our thoughts to paper—instead of merely talking about them—a process that implicitly suggests something binding, almost contractual.

But take it from a bootstrapper: Planning is essential. Failing to plan really is tantamount to planning to fail. Buildings are erected based on an architect's blueprint. Dresses are made from a pattern. Plans give our fantasies concrete substance. They help transform the vague pie in the sky to DVD/Surround sound. It's one thing to walk around saying, "I want an exciting career." It's quite another to sit down and force yourself to map out a strategy that says, "I want a career that involves travel, includes high-level responsibility, allows me to meet new people. And I will apply to these companies."

Of course, no plan is complete without a realistic review of the obstacles you may encounter. Planning can help you prepare for the potential problems you're sure to come up against along the way. Planning and preparation go hand in hand, one feeding off the other. When I decided I wanted to launch Akwaaba Mansion Bed and Breakfast five years ago, I began by visiting every bed-and-breakfast I possibly could in order to learn more about the business. Then I enrolled in a week-long aspiring innkeepers' course in Cape May, New Jersey, the East Coast capital of inns, where I could learn about the behind-the-scenes operations. Then I started looking for a potential property in my neighborhood to convert into an inn.

If you're the woman who likes to "go with the flow," maybe the idea of planning and preparing seems too rigid for you. You may be that same sister who doesn't want to read the directions before assembly, who prefers to "wing it" when traveling rather than buy and read a map, or who believes simply that God will take care of everything. Just remember that God helps those who help themselves. Crises are bound to come up—they're unavoidable. But with a plan you're prepared to weather many of them.

Persistence and Patience

Right about now some of you may be thinking, "I've mapped out plans before. I've tried the preparation route and still failed." That may be true. But what's important to recognize is that there's nothing magical to the process of success. It is above all just that, a process—one that is about evolution, not revolution. We achieve our goals in mini, bite-size increments. That is, if we remain committed. You must press on. When something knocks you on your behind, get up and try it over again, learning from your past mistakes. Persistence is the one element that quickly separates the doers from the dreamers.

If you have the strength to keep on keeping on, I guarantee that you will easily trump at least half of your competitors. Truly. Nothing can take the place of persistence. Think about it. Talent is no substitute for perseverance. How many talented people do you know who don't fully apply themselves and end up frustrated and unsuccessful? Even brains can't take the place of persistence. As the old folks used to say, the world is full of "educated fools"— people whose smarts do them little good in the game of life. I'm telling you, persistence and her twin sister patience are the bomb—the dynamic duo that promises success. Have you ever wondered why the adage "You can't keep a good woman down" is so often repeated? Because it's true.

The woman who keeps plugging and is willing to wait out opportunity is the woman who gets to the pot of gold. She's the sister who grabs the brass ring. To many on the outside, it may look as if the successful sister is simply lucky. I don't buy in to the notion of dumb luck. An opportunity that knocks on the door is useless unless a person who has planned, prepared, persisted, and waited patiently for that occasion is standing on the other side to answer the call.

If you dream of a career in real estate and I come to you and propose the investment of a lifetime, what good is it to you if all you've been doing is dreaming about it? You've got no capital, no collateral, and no clue. The sister who is going to be able to make hay is the one who not only has the dream but has been saving her money, studying the market, and is ready and able to build her portfolio.

Passion and Purpose

It's not enough merely to *want* to achieve your goals; you need to have a burning insatiable hunger to achieve them. As you can see here and as you've no doubt learned throughout your own life, success is hard work. So why waste all that time and precious energy on something you can take or leave? When you review some of the goals you lay out, you may find there are dozens of things on your list. If that's the case, you need to pare down and focus. Go back and ask yourself as you examine each goal, "How badly do I want it?"

The things you want most to accomplish in life virtually have to consume you—overtake all other priorities. If you want to watch television or hang out at the club more than you want to put in the work needed to plan your destiny, then you'll obviously spend more time on those pursuits than you will living out your dreams. If you can live with that, fine. But I thought you were a bootstrapper.

That means you have passion and purpose—not just desire. In other words, you want to reach your goal with every fiber of your being, and you believe God put you on this earth to do so. Passion and purpose fuel your wants, propel your dreams into action. Together, they fire you up and motivate you to claim your destiny. No two people have exactly the same passion and purpose—even if they happen to share a dream. I believe that these two forces play out differently within each individual. For example, in my case, growing up in a home that was loving and warm—but fraught with financial insecurity—stirred a passion in me to achieve a measure of economic stability. It has informed my frugal lifestyle and set me on a course of investing and saving. For others, that same situation may have created a passion for fine clothes or fancy cars. Now, we both want to live large, but our passions differ dramatically.

Before you can see your dreams manifest, you must identify your passion and your purpose. The same as a carpenter needs his hammer and saw, these are the tools *you* need to build the things you desire.

Positive Role Models and Patting Yourself on the Back

A bootstrapper is out to do the unexpected—chart her own course, without the cushy connections of family members. It's a brave proposition. It's bold and it's admirable. But it can also be extremely tough, unless you look outside your immediate circle to find folks who can inspire you to achieve your heart's desire. Who do you know who is leading the kind of life you aspire to? A successful businesswoman? A high-powered sister-executive? A mom who seems to have the patience of Job? Seek out these positive role models. Do all you can to get close to them, to observe them and learn from them. In your own quest to excel, it will serve you well to receive guidance and support from those who have gone before you. These folks help to remind you that what you're trying to achieve is indeed doable. They put a human face on your dreams.

Your positive role models are not your only encouragement. It is also important that you become in effect your own cheerleader by occasionally giving yourself a hearty pat on the back. With all the challenges you face in your quest to succeed, you can ill afford to work against yourself by being overly critical or negative. As you go about your day, remember to talk yourself through any upsets you might encounter. For example, when you fall behind on a project, remind yourself of how well you perform under pressure and recall the times that you've pulled through tight deadlines before. This kind of self-talk is far more productive than beating yourself up with what I call the "If I–should've–could've–would've" paddle. What's done is done. Fill your head with positive-speak.

Chapter 2

SUCCESSFULLY DEFINING SUCCESS

$\mathcal{W}$hat is success anyway? It's what we all say we want. But how many of us are operating with a clear understanding of what success really means? Before you can achieve it, you must be able to define it for yourself.

If you were to draw a picture of your fine, successful self, what would it look like? Would you be in a demanding, high-profile career, earning the big bucks? Or would you have the J-O-B that pays a fair to middle-range salary but offers little stress and the bonus of free time? Would there be an adoring husband or several sexy suitors in your life? A quiet social life with a few close friends or a public one where everybody knows your name? I know a supertalented young sister who was presented with the opportunity to join the staff as second in command of a highly anticipated new magazine. She declined. Instead she opted to take the number-four position. Why? At twenty-eight years old she wants a high-flying career *and* a family. If she's busy running a major publication during her prime dating and mating years, how will she realize the second half of her dream?

Is sister-girl successful?

How about this self-assured woman I recently met? She was successfully navigating a career on the Information Superhighway before most of us even knew how to find the on-ramp. With a six-figure dot-com salary at stake, she left Silicon Valley and returned to her hometown of Bedford-Stuyvesant, Brooklyn, where she is plowing her wealth into the community by pitching stakes as an entrepreneur.

A success in your book?

Consider the thirty-something sister who, after having her first child, stepped off the corporate ladder to become a full-time mommy, cutting her household income by half. She decided she could return to a $75K salary and grueling work hours anytime, but her baby would only be a baby for a short time and she didn't want to miss it.

Does such a lifestyle spell S-U-C-C-E-S-S?

All three of these folks are winners in my book because success is personal fulfillment. But how many of us are trying to live out someone else's vision of success—one handed down by our parents or peers or by society?

The first step in achieving success is knowing in your heart of hearts what's important to you. That means knowing your inner self like the back of your hand. Be honest, when was the last time you sat down and had a good, long talk with you? It's a good idea to spend quiet time with yourself daily. Ask yourself what I call "core belief" questions.

✦   Do I like getting out of bed in the morning? Why or why not?

✦   What brings me joy? Really lights me up?

✦   What are the things I would *never* do?

✦   What makes me angry? (The answers to this question often reveal your passions.)

✦   In what ways am I special?

✦   What do I do better than just about anyone else I know?

✦   If I found out I only had one more day to live, what would I spend it doing?

Shhh . . . Be Still

If you ever hope to achieve your dreams, you have to do like that old Michael Jackson song—look at the (wo)man in the mirror. Is she bitter or joyful? Is she confused or centered? Empty or fulfilled? If you don't like something you see, don't be afraid to ask her to change her ways. At the end of the day, what matters most in life is not how the rest of the world regards you, it's how you feel about that sister staring back at you in the mirror.

Many of us would love to find the key to unlock the mysteries of our souls but simply don't know how. While the idea may seem daunting, the process is really not as difficult as you might think. The first thing you need to do is find some quiet time for yourself. This idea, of course, is not new. It is probably one of the simplest pieces of advice we receive when it comes to self-enlightenment. It is, in fact, so simple that I think it is easy at times to overlook its importance.

Try to think of it this way: Imagine how many thoughts we are forced to process throughout any given day. If you commute to work, you start the day with the maddening sounds of rush-hour traffic or screeching subway trains. Once you arrive at your job, there is a veritable cacophony of sound—from the almost constantly ringing telephone and fax machine to the hum of voices coming at you from all sides. Evening hours find many of us in front of the television set, where again we are assaulted by a rush of sound and sight. If you're the sister who falls asleep in front of the TV, all that clamor is incorporated into your subconscious. So even when your body should be at rest, your head is on full alert.

As you try to get closer to the ideal you, a few short moments of silence are not a throwaway piece of the puzzle. They are an absolute necessity. It is likely the only opportunity you will have throughout the chaos of your day to calm your senses, quiet the voices, and become still to the point where all you hear is the only voice that matters—your own.

Set aside at least fifteen to thirty minutes of stillness, preferably at the beginning and end of your day. Use this time to reflect on your feelings—on what makes you happy, what scares you or makes you anxious. Write your thoughts down in a journal. Through the act of recording your feelings, you will probably find that the positive things in your life are in far greater supply than you may have realized, and you have much to be grateful for. Savor these things. Give thought each day to how they enrich your life. Writing down the less-than-positive emotions you may be experiencing serves a useful purpose, too. Charting these things that may have taken on huge proportions in your mind is a great way of deconstructing them. Seeing the fact that you are fearful of getting hurt in a new relationship, for example, can help you confront that fear for what it is. You may come to see the fear, anger, or whatever emotion not as some crippling force of doom, but as a mere function of your uncertainty about a situation. The simple act of putting the feeling in black and white gives you an incredible sense of release.

You should also look to your periods of solitude as an exciting opportunity to tap into your dreams. Your imagination is a very powerful tool on your path to success and self-fulfillment. Think of your dreams as a great preview of your life's coming attractions.

Be fanatic about your quiet time to dream. If you can't afford fifteen minutes, give yourself ten, but don't let it go. If you do happen to let a day pass without it, quickly get yourself back on track the next. Think about it. You probably spend close to ten hours preparing for and working at your job each weekday. And we won't even begin to calculate the number of hours you devote to caring for your family and tending to your household and other chores. Aren't you yourself worth at least a fraction of that time? If you think you don't have the time, let me tell you that you simply can't afford not to make it.

That's not to suggest that this process will teach you everything there is to know about you. On the contrary, once you think you've got it all figured out, you become stagnant. You may reach a goal or two, but by neglecting to go deep within, out of fear, you resist change. And change is the only way we are able to grow. I'm not ashamed to say that I'm a work-in-progress. I think the smartest, most successful people in the world realize that they don't have it all figured out. But because they are on the road of self-discovery and open to the wonders of themselves, they are constantly surprising themselves, finding that they have more courage, more knowledge, and more strength than they ever knew.

Learning about your true self has an added bonus. It gives you confidence and inner strength. The more you get inside yourself, the more you realize just how special a creature you are. You will be totally unconcerned with the folks around you who are doing their thing because you will be so consumed with getting into your own groove. If I stopped to give weight to any talk swirling about me—you know, the "She thinks she's so . . ." kind of talk—

I would never complete half my work. There may be many who look at my life and the roles I juggle and say, "Wow, she's really hustling. She's trying to get paid."

Those people have got it only half right. I am hustling; I'm a hardworking sister. But I'm not trying to strike it rich. For me, making money is simply a means to an end—a way to make my family comfortable and help others. I'm not trying to be successful, because even without titles and press clippings, I know I am a success. And I have been for quite some time.

Let me back up before you think I'm ego-tripping. You see, when I was growing up, my parents never defined success for me. Instead I was always told that I would be successful in whatever I chose to do, and my choices were supported.

From the time I was a little girl, my every goal and aspiration was honored and respected. Some of you might recall the late-sixties show *Julia*. It was the first prime-time TV show to feature an African-American woman as a professional—Diahann Carroll playing a nurse. With everything in me at nine years old, I wanted to emulate this beautifully poised and successful black woman. Once I announced my nursing ambitions to my parents, I was outfitted in fairly short order with a toy stethoscope, medical bag, nursing cap, and navy cape.

When I decided in junior high school that I wanted to be a news anchor, my grandmother stepped up and said, "If that's the case, that child's going to need braces," and she put money aside each month from her meager Social Security check to foot the orthodontist's bill. Years later, as a college coed with the dream of becoming a fashion editor, I worked my way through Howard University as a reporter at the military newspaper *Stars & Stripes* during the summer and school breaks. After graduation I was offered a permanent position at the paper, which I summarily declined. I wanted a career in fashion journalism, and I knew that New York, not D.C., was where I had to go. Like most black men of his era, my father could not understand the idea of turning down a "good" government job—decent pay, benefits, and security. But he never tried to make me surrender my dream. He collected some used furniture and moved it—and me—to New York. I realize now how fortunate I was. My parents taught me at a young and crucial age one of the fundamental elements of success: claiming what you want.

Claiming Yours

You cannot realize your vision of success until you are able to actually visualize yourself as successful. Once you see that image clearly and purposefully, you then must believe you have the power to be it. That's where many of us drop the ball. In your daydreams, you may identify yourself as a confident, fulfilled sister: She's doing work she enjoys, loving a beautiful brother, and being loved in return. Perhaps she's traveling the world in fine clothes or just spending quality time with her kids or gardening in her own lush backyard. But if you're like many sisters, the traffic light changes or the phone rings and you snap out of the daydream, then tell yourself to get real.

Let me tell you, that daydream was real—it was your real-life vision of success. And in order to achieve it, you've got to summon the power to claim it. After all, happiness is your birthright. There are some who believe suffering is synonymous with being a good Christian. Such folks actually think it's wrong to pray anything except "pleading" prayers that ask God to give them something. By claiming, you are, in effect, affirming that He has already blessed you with what you want. You are declaring to the universe that you are ready to receive what you deserve.

You need to check yourself if you find yourself claiming your good when you stop to pray at night but spend much of the day casting off your daydreams as out of reach. There is an intrinsic connection between thoughts, words, and actions. It has been proven that people with winning attitudes—in other words, those who expect good things to happen—actually experience greater success. Your thoughts have a huge influence on your future. Positive and affirming thoughts keep you open, prepared, and able to accept the fabulous opportunities that come your way.

Once you have truly claimed your good, there is no turning back. After affirming over and over again that your destiny is yours, you simply cannot go back to the doubting and second-guessing that may have consumed your preclaim days. I don't mean to suggest that claiming has some magical powers that will make your wildest dreams come true with a wave of a hand. There will still be challenges to overcome.

Staring Down the Opposition

Here is the beauty of claiming what you want. When you see that vision oh-so-clearly, you begin to realize that no one can take it away. You become focused on what you truly want out of life, and when a stumbling block presents itself, you realize that it's only an opportunity to demonstrate how strong your determination really is.

I know. I'm a witness. Back in 1994, my husband, Glenn, and I purchased our dream home in Stuyvesant Heights, Brooklyn. The beautiful eighteen-room mansion was a couple of blocks away from the brownstone we'd been living in for the past five years. I'd walked by this incredible Italianate structure countless times, picturing myself and my family living inside its grand walls. One day I decided to ring the bell to see if there was any chance the owners wanted to sell. No answer. So I slipped a note under the door, with my phone number on it, asking about the possibility of buying the property. No call.

Then, after a year of leaving frequent notes and knocking on the unanswered door, I happened to see a very unassuming man standing in the yard. I screeched my car to the curb and jumped out. The man explained that this was his family home, and it had recently been damaged by a fire. Now he and his two sisters—all over the age of seventy—were looking for a buyer. Well, *I* was that buyer. I convinced my husband that we should go for it, and the next morning we were in contract. It took almost two years to close the deal because the sellers were caught up in some very messy estate matters. But on Thanksgiving eve two years later, we moved in, filled with the joy felt by all young couples when they settle into that wonderful place in which they plan to watch their children do everything—from playing in the yard to bringing home a prom date.

Beyond such dreams, Glenn and I had another goal—to be a beacon in our promising community by creating its first bed-and-breakfast. We had enjoyed our stays at quaint inns in Cape May, New Jersey, and other towns so much that we longed to bring our own Afrocentric flavor to a B&B set in the heart of Bedford-Stuyvesant. To us, this was a win-win for the neighborhood. We envisioned an oasis that would offer elegant but down-home accommodations to out-of-towners in the area visiting family and friends. In a place as big as Brooklyn—if it were a city rather than a borough, it would be the country's fourth largest—there was no major hotel at the time. But much more than a business where we put heads on beds, we saw ourselves creating something that would be a source of pride for our fellow Bedford-Stuyvesant residents. So we just knew everyone would be pleased and supportive once they learned of our plans. I guess we should have known better.

A handful of neighbors tried to whiteout our dream for Akwaaba Mansion Bed and Breakfast. A few were simply naysayers who couldn't fathom the idea of people coming to Bed-Stuy and spending their hard-earned money to stay at our inn. But far more dangerous were the few player haters, the sad, bitter black folks operating from the position that if they weren't happy and "successful," why should we be? They went so far as to instigate the temporary closing of our B&B for possible zoning violations. With most of the community behind us, we fought diligently—petitions, talk-radio interviews, candlelight prayer vigils, and top-notch legal and architectural consultation—and in the end, we won.

During this whole ordeal, we had begun to strategize. If the inn could not be, we could possibly open a fine restaurant in the neighborhood—another business the community sorely needed. Two years later, with the inn booked every weekend, we opened Akwaaba Cafe, a seventy-two-seat restaurant housed in a brownstone we owned down the street. Two years later, in the summer of 2000, we opened a coffeehouse in the multiple-unit building we purchased next door to the restaurant. Our daughter Glynn who was eight at the time, named the coffeehouse Mirrors. "I want there to be mirrors all over the place, so when our people come in, they can see their beauty," she said. I wept. At eight, she *got* it.

A hair salon and a barbershop were already doing a fine business in the building when we bought it. That left two vacant retail spaces—two more opportunities to deliver the kinds of services other neighborhoods took for granted. We looked around for other like-minded people who might want to be entrepreneurs and help develop the economic lifeline of the community. We found Crystal and Walston Bobb-Semple. Both under the age of thirty, they had lucrative day jobs but were willing to work hard and long hours to run their own businesses too. We gave them very low rent as an incentive to take the plunge.

Now Bedford-Stuyvesant has its very own general bookstore and an upscale antiques shop to boot.

True That

You see, I have a personal pledge that I live by: I refuse to be limited by other people's limited imaginations or expectations. There may have been many who doubted the success of a bed-and-breakfast or any such commercial strip in Bed-Stuy. In their minds, they saw certain facts: It's an all-black neighborhood, and many of its residents are struggling to make ends meet. The media has long depicted the community as one overwhelmed with crime, drugs, and hopelessness; and there has never been a B&B or anything like a general bookstore in the area.

These are, indeed, undeniable facts. I cannot argue that. But they were never *my* truths. And there is a difference. Jim Crow segregation and taxation without representation were facts of life for millions of African-Americans just a few decades ago. But brave civil-rights pioneers paved the way for equal access, and by 1964, the truth is—despite the odds—blacks were guaranteed the right to vote. Had we simply accepted the facts, imagine what our truth would be today. The Good Book says: "You shall know the truth and the truth will set you free." My friend, you must know your truth.

Once you do, listening to people who can't see your goals—people who are bound by facts, fear, jealousy, or just plain stupidity—will do you no good. Indeed, if you let it, such talk can trap you into a state of self-doubt and shortsightedness. And this is an especially dangerous situation for us sisters. We are extremely vulnerable to the perceptions others may have of us, often twisting ourselves into pretzels to make those around us feel comfortable and secure.

Think about it. How many people in your life are you trying to satisfy? Do you yearn to be an actor or an artist but instead continue to toil in a job that does little to satisfy you simply because that's what you prepared for in school and you don't want to "waste" the money your parents spent on education? Do you come home and cook dinner for your husband at night so he won't feel neglected, despite your unrelenting workday of back-to-back meetings and deadlines? Do you feign empathy when your girl is complaining for the umpteenth time that her true love has betrayed her once again?

If you've answered yes to any of these questions, in all likelihood you are suffering from the "disease to please." As women, we tend to shoulder more responsibility in relationships, making it very difficult in many cases to just say no. Even if it leaves us cursing under our breath, many of us go out of our way to be accommodating. We're quick to say, "Yeah, girl. I'll bring the potato salad," even though we've already been put in charge of the paper plates, ice, and plastic forks too. Generally, the need to meet—and even exceed—the expectations of those around you comes out of love. You may even think that by not indulging the needs of others you are somehow being selfish.

To be sure, there is nothing wrong with helping a sister (or a brother) out. But it becomes a problem when we develop a pattern of committing ourselves to things we really don't want to do. Family and friends can expect to receive your love and support, but not every last drop of your time and energy! When you take on too much responsibility for things that have little to do with you, in the process you leave yourself less time for those things that do matter. Trust me: There is no glory in selfless acts that keep you from your purpose. (To learn strategies for saying no, check out Chapter 3, "'Me' Time.")

If you are to stay on course, you must remain steadfast in

your focus. You must purge your life of the things that drain you and binge on those things that drive you. Basically, this means that you begin organizing your life in a way that reflects your priorities. If there's one thing I've mastered, it is this. In fact, it is part of the answer to the question I am often asked: "How do you do it all?" Most of us are completely unaware of just how many tasks we perform and things we experience that have absolutely nothing to do with our goals in life. Many of these distractions, however, we bring upon ourselves, either because we are not selfish about our time or because we don't realize where our time is being misspent. I make every minute count, and I can account for every minute.

I live by my daily to-do list, which I hand-write in a basic steno notepad. I write the list out at night for the next day, and often sketch out the next few days while I'm at it. Then, in the morning I review it to make sure I'm clear about what I intend to accomplish. I keep that list with me at all times, checking off each task as it's completed. The list is very detailed, organized by time slots. Sometimes I'm overly optimistic about what I can accomplish. But if something doesn't get done, I don't beat myself up about it. I simply move it to the next day.

I'm always mindful to schedule in a little time just for me, and I try to make sure it happens. The times when I have let it slide, I've ended up feeling resentful and edgy at the end of the day.

That leads me to the idea of emotional drains—those things that sap your energy and take you off purpose. These are the people, thoughts, or activities that do more than work your nerves. They slowly but surely deplete your emotional, spiritual, even physical energy.

Under the list of Emotional Drains, check all the items that apply to you, and feel free to add others that occur to you.

Emotional Drains

+ Many of my friends' conversations are filled with gossip and negative talk.

+ I know I would feel whole if only I had a man.

+ I'm in a relationship where my needs are not being met.

+ There's something about my physical appearance that bothers me.

+ My closets and drawers are junky and I can rarely find anything.

+ I know many of the foods I eat are no good for me.

+ I long to get quiet, but can never seem to find the time.

+ Because I can't figure out what to wear, or find my keys, I'm often running late.

+ At the end of most workdays I sit on the couch and watch TV all night.

+ On Sunday evenings, I dread the thought of another work week.

+ I'm overdue for a raise or promotion, but I've yet to speak up.

+ I spend more than I earn.

+ I have unpaid credit cards or school loans hanging over my head.

+ I don't save money regularly and have no long-term financial security.

Are you beginning to get an idea of where your energy is going? Cheryl Richardson, author of *Take Time for Your Life,* says most people have at least 75 percent of their mental energy tied up in these kinds of distractions. We all know that each and every action uses up energy. But what we may not realize is that even actions that we don't make exert much-needed energy—mental energy that could be directed more positively to help us achieve our goals.

Now that you are on your way toward recognizing what may be depleting your most valuable resources of time and energy, you can begin to think about change. As everyone who has ever attempted to make a change knows, it doesn't come easily. But change can and will happen if you commit yourself to the process. For me, one of the strongest tools for change is visualization.

Review some of the things that are draining you—misplacing your keys, for example. Now see yourself moving through your morning smoothly—keys at the ready when it's time to leave the house. You are calm, unharried, and organized—the exact opposite of what you experience now. After you have envisioned yourself in the constructive mind-set, develop a plan or think of some possible ways you might get there. Perhaps, instead of flinging your keys on the counter when you walk in, you might place them on a hook near the doorway for easy access. You might practice this routine every day until it becomes habit. Try this with all the things in your life that are the source of negative energy: Visualize. Plan. Act. Practice.

Start small. Those small accomplishments will give you the confidence and momentum you need to tackle the big things. Give yourself time. You didn't develop draining habits overnight, and you won't be able to conquer them in an instant. What's important is that you never stop trying.

In time, you will find yourself gradually moving away from things that drain you and toward the kind of things that drive your energy.

Emotional Drives

- ✦ I have a solid circle of progressive friends who recharge my spirits.

- ✦ I know the right man will love and honor me for who I am.

- ✦ My things are in order, and I keep them neat and orderly.

- ✦ My diet is balanced, and I've reduced my intake of sugar and caffeine.

- ✦ I make time to write in my journal and find solitude each day.

- ✦ At the end of the day, I usually feel energized and self-satisfied.

- ✦ I review my performance and discuss my career with my boss regularly.

- ✦ I rarely have unpaid credit-card balances, and I pay my bills on time.

- ✦ I save money monthly and invest in a retirement plan.

You may look at some of these statements and think they are just empty words. It may be hard to believe that you'll ever achieve such states of well-being. But words are very important to your path to success. Words are our vehicles for relating to reality. Once we start speaking in more positive terms, we are on our way to living those positive experiences. Think of your words not just as a way to communicate but also as a reflection of your state of mind. Quite simply, once you speak, you literally start to create your reality. Through speech you bring your thoughts to life. So be very mindful of what spews forth from your mouth.

And even in those times when you may not be experiencing the degree of success you might wish for, think and speak in the most positive language possible. One way to help get your mind attuned to the positive is through affirmation. Lots of spiritual teachers subscribe to the cosmic process of affirmations, but I like the very simple *Webster's* definition, which states that to affirm means to "make firm" or "to declare positively." In essence, using words as affirmations can transform us. I have turned many a tough day around by "affirming myself" out of a negative state and into a positive one. So believe me when I tell you there is power in affirming.

I believe there is no wrong or right way to affirm yourself. But to get the most out of your affirmations, I would suggest the following pointers to get you started.

✦ **AFFIRM IN THE HERE AND NOW.** State your affirmations in the present tense; for example, "I am whole. I am worthy."

✦ **MAKE IT PERSONAL.** Remember, you can only effect change in yourself, not in others or the outside world. So your affirmations should be self-centered, beginning with I. If a work or family turmoil has you troubled, you might say, "I am the calm in this storm. I shall not be moved."

✦ **KEEP IT POSITIVE.** Your goal with any affirmation is to channel the universe's positive forces. So avoid words like *won't, not,* and *don't.* If you want to avoid eating something you know is bad for you, tell yourself, "I am full."

✦ **BE DIRECT.** It's important that your affirmation be clear and simple. Look at the areas of your life and state your goals in a nutshell. If this seems like a monumental task, make one of your affirmations "I am decisive and forthright."

✦ **SAY IT AGAIN** (and again, and again). Affirmations need to be repeated often in order to change old habits and thoughts. It can help to put daily reminders in highly visible areas, such as your bathroom mirror, dashboard, and desk calendar.

Success Saboteurs

We've all been there before: stuck in neutral. In our efforts to move forward, we have seemingly done all the right things—identified our goals, set a plan, done our inner work. Still, something is not clicking. It is almost as though we are trapped in quicksand. Our legs and arms are flailing, but we're not getting anywhere. For example, you know that to get to the next level in your career, you need to become computer-savvy. You have sent away for the information booklets. You've even begun filling out the application. But another semester has come and gone, and you have yet to register. What's holding you back?

All of us bootstrappers want to claim our success. By our very natures, we are dissatisfied with the status quo—when we know in our hearts we can, and should, be doing better. But what does it take for a sister to go from talking the talk to walking the walk? How can we possibly reach our optimum success when a strange and agonizing *something* seems to be tugging at our heels?

I know. Most of it is not your fault, there were extenuating circumstances, like, you were going to start saving this month but then your girlfriend's baby shower came up. And you just *had* to get her that designer layette. After all, you and she go way back. And sure, after your most recent performance review you were planning to pull out the stops at work—start coming in a few minutes earlier, stop packing up at four-fifty each evening. But it's hard, because you and your friends in the department across the hall like to arrive at happy hour early to get a good seat at the bar.

You are not alone. We sisters are experts when it comes to what I call "success sabotage." Partly the result of self-esteem issues that keep us from recognizing our greatness and partly the effect of years of social and family messages that seem to say, "Stay in your place," we constantly sabotage ourselves. We dream about success and we talk about success, but—usually on a sub-conscious level—we do almost everything within our power to see that it never happens.

As with any unhealthy behavior, the first step toward remedy is admission. Take a cold, hard look at where you are right now. How does what you say reconcile with what you do? If the two are at odds, it's time to stop the madness.

Tell yourself today "No More Excuses!" Don't start telling yourself (and the rest of the world) what you are *trying* to do. There is something called the law of least resistance. In other words, flowers don't try to grow—they simply grow. Water doesn't try to be wet—it simply is.

If you are ready to get to the heart of what is holding you back, read on. I spoke to some of the best sister therapists in the field to help you figure out what might be keeping you from moving forward.

Fear Factor

No one likes to admit it, but a sneaky four-letter word is lurking behind most of our excuses. It is pure unadulterated fear. There is a natural fear of the unknown. And even though we say we want our lives to change and move in a different direction, the fact is, we don't know what that new world will feel like. Will we change in some way? Will we have the same friends? Will our loved ones relate to us in the same way? All of these unknowns can be intimidating.

"There is both a fear of failure and a fear of success at work," says Dr. Grace Cornish, author of *10 Good Choices That Empower Black Women's Lives*. "If we succeed, there may be a ne~~ ~~le to adjust to. And if we fail, everyone will laugh at us."

Cornish notes that sisters have long heeded the

our childhoods—messages that said, "Don't show off," "You must think you're white," or "You think you're cute." What many of us came to internalize, as a result, was a mind-set that discouraged striving and, in effect, put a low premium on the work and drive needed to achieve success. To be safe and not offend others in our family or communities, we try not to stand out but to go along and get along with what the world expects of us.

To overcome those childhood messages, Cornish makes several recommendations. As we've been discussing all along, she says that we as black women have to take another look at what we call "success" so that we have our own definition—not society's. We need to first distinguish success—which is measured by outside sources—from "success-full," which is satisfying our inner longings for ourselves. Success for one sister might be defined as having a palatial house and a late model luxury car. Meanwhile, the sister who is living her dream of being a social worker and helping others, and has a loving circle of family and friends and money in the bank, is success-full. In other words, by fulfilling her own goals she is full of success even if she lives in a studio apartment and drives a wreck.

On the road to success, Cornish says, what trips many of us up are the three Cs: comparing, copying, and competing. We look around at others and see their externals—nice clothes, so-called glamorous jobs—and we say, "How come she's got it so easy and I don't?" Then, rather than live by our own internal standards of success, we use that sister as our measuring stick. Whether or not we can afford it, we try to copy her high style—drowning ourselves in debt in the process. Sometimes we even try to outdress her—almost as a way of assuring ourselves that we are just as good as she is.

"We need to say to ourselves 'Am I doing my best?' and not worry about the sister next to us," says Cornish. That takes self-discipline—doing what you need to do, even when you don't feel like it. Anything you do enough simply has to have definite consequences; it's universal law.

Blame Game

Okay, so we are the double minority and life is not fair. But who ever said it was going to be? Life is not fair for anyone. Besides, would you ever trade being a black woman for anything else? I didn't think so.

Yet that doesn't stop some of us from sitting around playing the blame game. You know how it goes: "This person or that situation conspired against me." "My mama (or daddy) did this to me." In short, in the blame game we are not accountable for anything that happens to us. Whatever goes wrong is the fault of myriad outside forces, all beyond our control.

"Blaming is a crutch," says Erline Belton, success coach and author of *Living on Purpose*, a guide to finding one's life vocation. "And we sisters need to throw down crutches and learn to walk." The reason we don't is clear, says Belton: We are afraid to confront who we really are—afraid of going beyond the superficial to the internal core. Sisters who blame constantly have usually failed to develop the habits of introspection needed to fulfill their goals. Blaming helps us hide from our souls. It often comes from anger that has been suppressed over time. And that anger, which comes from a place very deep inside us, originates from hurt. Blaming is a self-defense mechanism that keeps us from understanding our true purpose in life.

God put us all on the earth for a specific reason, and the longer we are able to keep from discovering it, the longer we can put off the work we're supposed to be doing. The self-enlightenment we all need to experience cannot be achieved when we are stuck in a blaming mode. That's because the blaming voices can effectively shut out the process of our getting still, as we talked about at the beginning of this chapter. Belton agrees that quiet meditation and prayer are "critically important" to finding our purpose in life.

And living with purpose is successful living. It is, of course, what we strive for—that sense of inner peace that comes from a place of total contentment and fulfillment. And while most of us realize that blaming doesn't solve anything, we sometimes feel powerless to stop it. We are largely not even aware that we are doing it. Rather than blame society, our parents, employers, and the like, Belton recommends we sisters should begin to have a different kind of conversation with ourselves. Instead of looking on the outside, we should begin by looking inward and asking the following:

✦　What hurts me?

✦　What am I afraid of?

✦　How do I recover from failures?

✦　What can I learn from others?

Woe Is Me—The Victim

The flip side to that worn-out blaming record is the victim song. Like blamers, victims are held back by a bevy of external forces—all debilitating and virtually impossible to overcome. Of course, none of us sisters are really victims. Our foremothers endured the Middle Passage, slavery, Jim Crow segregation, violence, and oppression and still managed to overcome.

Yet according to sister-therapist Dr. Brenda Wade, author of *What Mama Couldn't Tell Us About Love,* what some of us do is make ourselves victims. She tells the story of a very well-off sister-entrepreneur who owns and runs her own auto dealership, lives in a fine house, and drives a Rolls-Royce. Any given month, this "successful" woman can be found tearing along the highway, rushing to get to the utilities payment center before they cut off her electricity.

Wade says that despite lives filled with more privilege than previous generations could ever have imagined, we sometimes create a damning cycle of behavior that holds us back from the success we seek. It varies for each woman. Some of us overeat, some overspend, while others overextend themselves physically so that they are always late and harried. This type of self-destructiveness stems from the fact that, as a people, we are suffering from Post-traumatic Slavery Disorder, according to Wade and many other psychologists. Depending on your age, the theory goes, you are only a few generations away from slavery and its dehumanizing effects. So the rage and inferiority messages are still buried in our psyches. "We have to find ways to heal the history," says Wade. "Because real success lies in believing that you deserve it." Exactly.

Chapter 3

"ME" TIME

I didn't grow up with one of those mothers who had beautiful perfume bottles and powder puffs on her dresser. My mother didn't luxuriate in a sweet-smelling bubble bath at night, nor did she have a standing appointment at the beauty parlor.

What Mama did have was a strong work ethic. When all five of us kids were finally settled in elementary school—I was about eleven—she went back to work as a microfilm machine operator in the afternoons from three-thirty until midnight, after having sent us off to school, made beds, washed clothes, cooked dinner, and handled bills during the day. The next morning she woke up at seven and started the whole process over again.

They say the apple doesn't fall far from the tree. In my case its true. I've spent much of my career in the very hedonistic world of women's beauty and fashion. Each month in the magazines I've worked for, we proffer advice on the mind/soul/body benefits of the latest and greatest in everything from fitness routines, like yoga and tai chi, to beauty treatments, like mud facials and body wraps. Still, I hardly qualified as an expert on any of these feel-good tacks, because I rarely took the time to experience any of them firsthand.

To make matters worse, I would leave the office each night—often very late—and go home to work at the bed-and-breakfast. There, I found the paying guests cooling out—enjoying conversation, sitting by *my* fireplace, sipping *my* tea. Some days I went about the evening's duties—returning telephone inquiries, turning down beds, and prepping for the next morning's breakfast—with a tinge of resentment. I thought, "Here I am working like a dog, and they're just sitting around maxing and relaxing and enjoying my house." Something was clearly wrong with my outlook. The guests were doing exactly what they were supposed to do. My frustration was about my not doing what I needed to do—nurture myself.

I began to realize that my own learned habits of self-neglect had forced "me" time to the dead last slot on my to-do list. Somehow everything I had going on seemed more pressing—somehow more important—than taking care of me. Even as recently as a year ago, when the conceptualization of this book began, I'd relegated this section on self-care to being the next-to-last chapter! Imagine that. A book on success and fulfillment in which looking after numero uno is nearly an afterthought.

The lightbulb went off around my fortieth birthday. I had planned to throw a big party, but then reconsidered. That again would be a lot of people having a good time at my expense. With this book project weighing heavily on my mind, I went away instead—sans the husband and daughter—for a restorative weekend by the beach. I took along my laptop just in case I got inspired to begin the book. It was as though someone had turned on the water faucet of my brain. All of the thoughts I'd been struggling to pull together for the past year suddenly began to pour out of me. I "saw" the book unfolding in perfect order, chapter by chapter. I labored not. I stressed not. It simply flowed. Then I got toward the end of my weekend project—thoroughly outlining each chapter—and it hit me: Self-care, or pampering, is where it all begins. It should be a priority, born not out of selfishness or egotism but out of healthy self-love and self-support.

The Strong Black Woman Syndrome

I realized that I was probably not so different from every other black woman, juggling myriad roles. But whether we know it or not, "me time" is something almost every sister is in desperate need of. We come from a culture in which we as black women are expected to take on a dizzying burden of responsibility. Our mothers did it, as their mothers did before them. But unlike the slave-era matriarchs, whose men were forcibly removed from the family, we are not solely responsible for holding up the race. Today the practical necessity of being Strong Black Women is not as pressing. Yet, whether out of guilt, obligation, or habit, few of us modern-day sisters step up to break the cycle. Regarded as the pillars of the family, the church, the community, we are cornered into a lifestyle so filled with serving others that there's little room for restoring ourselves. Those around us—husbands, friends, co-workers—come to see us as superhuman beings who have no such earthly needs. And we never dream of asking for assistance, because we've already elevated the needs of everyone else above our own.

Like most Americans in this media-driven society, sisters have bought in to the notion that success is virtually synonymous with hectic, overextended living. In his book *Don't Sweat the Small Stuff . . . and it's all small stuff*, Richard Carlson notes that by living a frantic lifestyle that denies your inner needs, "you literally immobilize yourself from your greatest potential." We sometimes wear our stress like a badge of honor, too. Does the following exchange sound familiar?

"Hey, girlfriend, how ya living?"

"Crazy, honey."

"You and me both."

What typically follows is laughter, a few nods and maybe a sister-to-sister high five. We accept being worn out and dragged down as the norm. It doesn't have to be that way.

I began to look ever more closely at my own self-care habits. In a life filled with so much activity and responsibility, there seemed to be precious little "me" time. I really examined some of the ways I spent my downtime. I could look back with pride on the founding of the Go On, Girl! Book Club, a group launched from a real need to carve out more quality time with my best girlfriends. Back in 1991, I, along with Lynda Johnson and Tracy Mitchell-Brown, began with the simple notion of having a regular activity to bring us and a few other friends together socially. We chose the name Go On, Girl! purposefully to affirm our friendship and ourselves. We decided to gather at each other's homes monthly to read topical books, have lively discussion, and just vibe in the warm comfort of each other's company. Usually our book talk about prose, theme, and protagonist segued into girl talk about life, men, whatever. And often the afternoons melted into evenings. Our group grew nationally to include chapters in twelve states. Now there are thirty such chapters boasting a total of some four hundred sisters—the largest reading group for black women in the country! I am the national president, and there are board meetings, bylaws, newsletters, logo merchandise, and an annual conference. While I love all that the book club is, when it started to feel a little like work instead of "me" time, I needed to identify another breakaway pastime.

Transforming Might and Spirit

I'm proud to say that in the past year or so I've found what is probably the single most gratifying "me" commitment I've made thus far: my fitness routine. I'm not going to lie to you. Since I began working out regularly, I'm loving the body I'm in—not just because my size-twelve frame is trimmer and my husband thinks I'm all that, but because I know this is the best me I can be. I can climb subway stairs without getting winded. I can play alongside my daughter, Glynn (for a little while at least), without feeling like an old bag of bones. And I can pull clothes out of my closet in the morning with confidence instead of the uneasy hesitation of wondering which outfit best hides which body part.

But easily the most satisfying feeling of all comes from those sacred sixty to ninety fitness minutes of oneness with myself. The actions of my body somehow magically work to transform my mind and my spirit. I'm filled with a sense of control and accomplishment that is quite unlike anything I've ever experienced. Don't be confused. I'm no Jackie-Joyner Kersee or Marion Jones. But when I'm working out, I feel as though I can definitely identify with that "high" that top athletes often describe. And it's no wonder. Scientists have proven that exercise prompts the body to release a certain feel-good hormone, called seratonin. It's the same chemical reaction ignited by drugs like Prozac, prescribed to treat people suffering from depression. My devotion to fitness has taught me an invaluable lesson: Sometimes what's good *for* you is also good *to* you. Exercising truly brings me joy.

Notice I said "brings me joy," not "makes me happy." There's an important difference. Sister Debrena Jackson Gandy teaches us in her book *Sacred Pampering Principles* that true pampering experiences come from within. Unlike the Westernized pursuit of happiness that looks for something to make you happy or cause you to become pleased, that which "brings you joy" comes from a deeper, internal point of reference.

"An experience that brings you joy brings you to a place within yourself that is the source of your joy," Gandy maintains. It is the difference between something that happens to you and something that happens in you. For example, buying a new pair of shoes might make you happy. It is something external that causes a certain amount of temporary pleasure. On the other hand, an activity such as gardening or knitting can trigger some kind of inner reaction—bringing you peace and joy. It is a more enduring feeling of contentment than an external or fleeting experience.

With that said, I must admit that, like most of us, I have a way to go when it comes to fully embracing the tenets of pampering and self-care. I, too, sometimes buckle under the weight of being a Strong Black Woman. For most of my forty years I have felt as though I was almost solely responsible for the well-being of those around me. From the time I was in second grade, I was the one who was put in charge of the class when the teacher stepped away. While not the eldest of my siblings, I am the firstborn female in a family of five children. As the saying goes, "Mothers love their sons and raise their daughters." Our society allows male children to fall into mischief (after all, "Boys will be boys"). But there's no such comfort zone for girls. There's no room for trifling or irresponsible behavior. It is expected that we will be dutiful, kind, and obedient. Thus, we are. If such roles come at the expense of our own fulfillment, so be it; that has been the attitude. I'm sure my experiences as woman child of our clan were not so different from your own.

In all my travels and talks with sisters, I think I have yet to meet one who wasn't struggling to somehow reconcile her own innermost desires with the demands of her Strong Black Woman–ness. Many of us are enduring the struggle with little or no awareness. In other words, we go through our daily lives dominating, not submitting; giving, rarely getting; doing, never delegating; and constantly answering the needs of others without asking for assistance even when we truly need a helping hand. In turn, our men, our friends, our fellow church members, even our families keep taking—not because they're terrible people, but because we have conditioned them to sit back and let us take care of everything.

Even when we hit bottom, reach the point where we are drained both physically and emotionally, many of us still fail to recognize the self-made trap in which we are ensnared. So we lash out at our families for being ingrates, at our men for being inconsiderate, at our co-workers or subordinates for being lazy. We grow resentful of these people around us. Then we blame them for the fact that we haven't had time to get a manicure in six months, haven't had time to got to the hairdresser regularly, haven't even had time to sit on the toilet and hear ourselves think for a minute.

Interestingly enough, no matter how angry we get at others, our behavior rarely seems to change. Sure, for a day or so we walk around with our mouths poked out—some of us sulk silently, others march around the house making grand pronouncements: "There're gonna be some changes around here!"

Am I talking to you? Don't be mad at me, sister. I'm really talking to us all—myself included (especially myself)! Just to show you how far gone I was at one point, I'll share a story with you. My daughter was watching a program on television one day (I rarely watch the tube myself), when I happened to pass by and catch a glimpse of a commercial promoting what I thought at the time to be an ingenious new product. It was a moisturizing lotion that you sprayed on your body. I can't remember the name of it now, but the commercial touted how you could cover your whole body in a jiffy with just a few squirts. I thought "Wow! That would really shave time off of my morning routine." (You know we sisters can't completely cut out applying lotion; otherwise we'll end up ashy by the time we get to work.) I made a mental note to pick up this new spray-on moisturizer. But by the time I reached the stairwell, it struck me to what depths I'd fallen. In order to squeeze an extra five minutes out of the morning, I was willing to deny myself my own touch during the one ritual of my entire day that allows for some measure of pampering. How pathetic! Once I came to my senses, I realized that, if anything, I should be trying to get more, not fewer, moments of self-care.

For many of us, taking several hours out of the week or setting aside the money to enjoy some kind of beauty treatment may not seem realistic. That simply means we need to become creative and invent inexpensive ways to grab moments of "me" time. Look at your daily round of activities. Where can you "steal" a few minutes that are yours alone to replenish your soul with some nurturing? Here are a few ideas:

✦ **HAPPY HOUR.** I'm not suggesting you hit your favorite watering hole for some two-for-one specials. I'm talking about creating a few moments for your own mood-enhancing time. If, for example, your energy typically begins to wane at about four in the afternoon, make that your "happy hour"—or at least happy fifteen minutes. Leave your workplace, if possible, and take a brief walk. If you have your own office, close your door and hold all calls. Then treat yourself to a soothing cup of herbal tea.

✦ **JOURNALING.** For me, nothing beats this relatively simple way of reconnecting to myself. There's something inherently cathartic about the act of recording your thoughts—whether they be the deepest secrets of life or the mundane whatnots that combine to give meaning to your very existence. You can keep one journal or many for different uses—tracking your travels, charting your blessings, or memorializing a transitory phase, like a pregnancy or engagement.

✦ **EARLY CALL.** For some sisters, the very idea of rising even a minute earlier than necessary is totally unfathomable. But believe me, it does have its benefits. When you begin your day by pounding the snooze button on your alarm clock, then making a mad dash to work—where, presumably, very little time is your own—you rob yourself of what could be a very peaceful and soul-centering time. Before your kids, your honey, or your roommate wakes up, take just twenty minutes or so of thoughtful repose—when you can pray and affirm your goals—to brace yourself for the hectic activities that lie ahead.

✦ **NIGHT CREEPING.** If you're absolutely not a morning person, you can get many of the same benefits of early reflection after hours. So many of us while away our spare time in the evenings in front of the television, even letting it hum us to sleep. This is a dangerous habit. To be sure, there are many worthwhile programs on TV. But in this age of urgent e-mails, faxes, and cell calls, enough is enough. Without even realizing it, the Information Age overload can bring on stress. Break free of the tube at a reasonable hour and, instead of the shrill of the evening news, fill your dreams with the much more pleasant silence of your own thoughts.

✦ **FEELING THE EARTH.** Nature has amazing restorative powers. Take advantage of any opportunity your life presents to get closer to the creator of all the splendor nature holds. Till a patch of soil in your backyard to create a wonderful flower or vegetable garden. If you don't have a yard, plant a window box of goodies. You might grow herbs or just pot some beautiful blossoms, but either way you will find yourself transformed by the experience.

If you're like me, when you see these ideas in black and white, they all probably seem easily doable. Still, at the end of the day most of us hit the bed with a thud—feeling totally whupped. We don't know where the day has gone. We don't understand why—with nearly eighteen waking hours—we have had not even one minute to ourselves; nor do we "get" the fact that the selfless-centered life model we labor under binds us to repeat the cycle day in and day out. You may not be able to turn it on its ear overnight, but you'd better at least recognize the reality. Not only is this mad compulsion unhealthy, it systematically usurps us of our personal power and self-esteem. What's more, in the end it undermines our efforts to nurture others. After all, if I can't bring myself joy and fulfillment, I can't possibly share those feelings with someone else.

So what do we do about it? We begin by falling in love with ourselves first and foremost, inside and out. Notice I'm not suggesting you merely *love* yourself. I want you to be *in love* with yourself, to the point where you shower yourself with the kind of warmth and attention heretofore reserved for your sexy soul mate. Massage your body with sensual, fragrant oils. Eat from your finest china. Sleep on your softest sheets. Give yourself the kinds of gifts you bestow on your best friends—pretty lingerie, a day of beauty at the spa.

This kind of pampering is, of course, learned behavior for most of us. We're not accustomed to breaking out the good, special-occasion stuff unless we're having company. Even working in the fashion and beauty industry for as long as I have, *I* hardly have these self-care principles down. If you don't believe me, think back if you can to my original photograph on the editor's page of *Essence*. You might recall how in the photo my hands are tucked neatly under my chin. Well, it wasn't because I was going for the coy, coquettish look. My nails and cuticles were crying out for a manicure, and since I couldn't find the time to get one, I didn't dare show my raggedy hands!

I have a way to go when it comes to fully embracing the pampering ethic. And I'm reminded of that fact every time I talk to my friend Mikki Taylor, the very mistress of self-care, and *Essence*'s beauty director. We probably all know of women like Mikki. This is a sister who—with standing nail, hair, and facial appointments—looks fabulous and has the youthful glow someone fifteen years her junior would envy. Her secret is really no secret at all. She'll tell anyone: "Treat your body like the temple it is." And she lives by that edict. Women like Mikki must know they look good. But what I've found is that for most world-class pamperers, what we—the world—see on the outside is only a fringe by-product of self-care. The real payoff is on the inside.

Anyone who looks at Mikki can see that she loves herself enough to honor herself. She walks with confidence and smiles easily. Whether she is all dolled up in evening clothes or wearing a simple sweater and a pair of slacks, she looks graceful and beautiful, because she has taken the time to self-nurture.

I appreciate Mikki and her gentle reminders to me to honor myself with the newest in facial treatments or aromatherapy candles. And I have come to realize that what she is encouraging me and others to do dates way back—to even before the dawn of the Strong Black Woman.

In ancient Egypt, women massaged their bodies with scented oils to keep their skin soft and supple. They used the mud of the

Nile to treat themselves to facials, and herbal extracts from plants to soothe their bodies. The Bible speaks of how "ointment and perfume rejoice the heart" and of women perfuming their beds with myrrh, aloes, and cinnamon.

As readily as we have embraced obligation, burden, and sacrifice—in the names of our families and our communities—we need to embrace joy and pleasure. Pampering is the first step in that process. It can unlock your ability to see the world differently—from a joyous center, rather than from a point of struggle. Like a ripple in a pond, this shift in mind-set then spills over into all areas of your life—your friendships, your self-image, your physical appearance, your romantic relationships, and your family interactions.

What you do to your body has a direct influence on the health and well-being of your spirit and your mind. When you tap in to the joys of life, you instantly provide nourishment to your spirit. And when you treat your body like the temple that it is, goodness and joy flow through all you give and all you receive. Make time to honor yourself, not by adding more and more duties to your already jammed to-do list but by approaching "me" time as another way to show love and appreciation. At the end of the day that is what self-care is all about—you giving back to you.

The (Gentle) Art of Saying "No"

One of the primary rules of giving back to you is to guard yourself vigorously against those forces that take from you in the first place. In other words, learn to honor yourself by honoring your time and your energy. That may mean saying no. It's a very short, simple, one-syllable word, but for some reason it's one of the most difficult to say. Most of us are not comfortable with rejection, and we're reluctant to risk hurting others with the powerful N word.

So instead we say yes to things we'd rather not do with people we'd rather not see.

Saying no becomes much easier the more you practice. If you're Miss Go-Along-to-Get-Along, it might be a good idea for you to begin with small doses of no's. For instance, if a saleswoman at the makeup counter has spent an hour with you going over the finer points of makeup and skin care, don't be guilted into buying a lipstick or some such item merely because she insists it looks fabulous. Just say no. It's one thing, of course, to say no to a salesperson you never have to see again; it's quite another to say it to family and friends.

Here are some basic rules.

+ **"JUST BECAUSE" IS SUFFICIENT.** Many of us don't say no more often because we don't feel we have good reason to. The truth is, you don't need a "good" reason; not wanting to do something is reason enough. Maybe you want to spend a quiet evening curled up with a book you've been meaning to read, or maybe you want to give yourself a pedicure. Remember that the whole point is to preserve as much "me" time as possible, and you can't do that if you're constantly pulled in a dozen different directions.

+ **KEEP IT SIMPLE.** Don't go into a whole bunch of detail when you let someone down. A simple "Sorry. I won't be able to" or "No. I can't. I have plans" (even if those "plans" amount to an evening spent in a relaxing bubble bath) will suffice. With some people, the more you try to justify the no, the more comebacks they will offer to get you to say yes. By the same token, an elaborate tale will most likely come back to bite you. Someone who really wants you to agree to something can usually pick apart a lie a lot quicker than you can weave one together. So don't bother.

✦ **BUY SOME TIME.** The best way to avoid commitment overload is to give yourself some time before coming up with a
response to invitations and requests. Sure, it's a bit of a cop-
out, but if done correctly it is a very polite way to cover yourself. Get comfortable with a few of these time-buying
standards:

"I need to check my calendar; I'll get back to you."

"I've got to think about that; I'll let you know."

"I think my husband/partner and I are going out that
night; I need to check with him first."

Be careful with these strategies. You can't use them
all the time. And unless you want to come across as a
flake, follow-up is a must. Get back to people in a timely
fashion, then bow out diplomatically.

I know that the Strong Black Woman in you is probably cring-
ing at the thought of studying how to say no. It probably seems
selfish, maybe even mean-spirited and conniving to methodically
develop ways to get out of helping those you care about. But try to
look at it another way. How often do you take on things—either
professionally or personally—out of obligation rather than love?
Midway through that project or task, you inevitably find yourself
becoming angry or resentful, don't you? Once you learn how to
say no without guilt, you will find yourself giving from a place of
generosity and warmth.

The more you say no to things that you have little time or
desire to do, the more you will be able to say yes to those experiences that give you the most joy. And isn't that our objective in
life? When you're getting what you need emotionally—when
you're fulfilled spiritually—you're in a far better position to reach
out to those around you with compassion and love. Only by saying
no to certain situations can you be effective and energetic to the
people, organizations, and causes you find meaningful.

Twenty-one Ways to Give Yourself to Yourself

1. Laugh as often as humanly possible.

2. Run through the sprinkler on a hot day.

3. Take in a movie in the middle of the afternoon.

4. Keep a set of dishes at work and eat from real plates the next time you order in.

5. Soak your feet in fragrant oils.

6. Curl up with a good book.

7. Prepare a romantic dinner for one—you.

8. Buy yourself fresh flowers and arrange them in a beautiful vase.

9. Luxuriate in a Jacuzzi or hot tub.

10. Take an early-morning walk on the beach.

11. Enjoy the sunset with a glass of wine or your favorite tea.

12. Make and keep regular massage appointments.

13. Place fragrant sachets in your lingerie drawer.

14. Turn off the phone ringer and let the machine pick up one evening.

15. Write yourself a love letter, seal it, and open it the next time you need a lift.

16. Light candles and walk around your house in the nude.

17. Buy a set of satin or silky sheets, just for you.

18. Break open a split of champagne and toast yourself.

19. Eat chocolate-covered strawberries in a warm bath.

20. Stay in bed all morning one Saturday.

21. Hug yourself today.

Chapter 4

A GREAT CAREER

*P*icture this. I'm fourteen years old. Every day after school, like a quick-change artist, I take off my fly gear—tight polyester bell-bottom pants and matching shirt—and put on my Wild, Wild West uniform. I trade my stylish platform shoes for a pair of cowboy boots and squeeze my huge afro puffs into a ten-gallon hat.

Once the outfit is hooked up, I greet my Roy Rogers customers—many of them friends from school—with these words: "Howdy there, partner. May I take your order?" Once they've finished laughing long enough to put in requests for burgers and fries or some such, out comes my follow-up: "Will you be eating that here or on the range?"

Corny? Sure, it was. But I wasn't fazed. I wore my silly getup with pride and performed my duties as a fast-food server with evangelical zeal. The fifty-dollars bonus for the Employee of the Month was mine just about every month.

Despite my schoolmates' snickers and ribbings, embarrassment or humiliation never crossed my mind. I felt that if I took a job as one of Roy's gals, then I was going to be a cowhand to the nth degree. Many years and many job titles later, that work ethic has remained intact. It's the bootstrapper in me.

Bootstrappers recognize that what is good for your job and what suits you personally are often contradictory. And that's okay. The bootstrapper in me also knows that the only thing that separates prosperous people from those who aren't prosperous is a readiness to work—really, really hard to do a good job.

There are those sisters who agonize over every career move. Let me be the first to tell you that if you haven't reached a point of some authority and weight in your field, you should consider just about any job as a way to inch yourself closer to your goal. That's the way success happens—inch by inch. It is a slow and often tedious process. And it's cumulative. As legendary *Cosmo* editor Helen Gurley Brown once said, success comes "sneaking in on little cat feet simply because you gave the best you could day after day, week after week, year after year."

It's Not Where You Are, It's Where You're Going

The way I see it, even if you don't particularly enjoy it, work can serve you in several different ways—all of them honorable.

✦ The position you hold right now may be the culmination of a lifelong dream. You have no trouble putting in ten- to fourteen-hour days, because it is your chosen vocation—the reason you leap out of bed every morning, eager to greet the coming day. If this is so, God bless you, my sister. You have found your calling.

✦ Maybe your current job is a stepping-stone on the road to a rewarding and promising career goal. Like a sponge, you spend each day soaking up the skills you'll need to move forward, and you're enthused with the prospect of a great future. If this is you, keep humping, girlfriend. Your dreams are within reach.

✦ Okay. So the job you hold right now is not turning you on. Sure, in the beginning you looked forward to the opportunities it would provide. But you realize now that it does not challenge your mind or motivate your spirit. This job is nothing more than a steady paycheck. Sound familiar? This may be you—and millions of other sisters. Let there be no shame in your game. Oftentimes a job is simply a means to an end, a way to pay your bills, finance a business or education, or afford you with some of life's pleasures.

Figure out where you are right now and take it for what it's worth. Whatever you may find unappealing in it, your job can in fact help you discover more about yourself.

Waiting for the perfect job is like waiting for the perfect life; there's no such thing. So while you hold out for the ideal job, why not try to change the one thing you can actually control—yourself. Before you head for the exit, try to come to an understanding about the place you're in now and find the value in it. Ask yourself, How can this—difficult boss or seemingly mindless work—make me grow in some way? What can I learn from it?

There's probably not a sister among us who hasn't had to suffer under a hard-driving boss—one who we felt was unnecessarily mean or unfair. But you cannot let such a person win—can't let him control your moods or dampen your ambitions. No, you have to figure out a way to get along with him. Think about it, in the end, it is that "impossible" boss who teaches you the most about tolerance and growth. And when *you* rise to a similar position of power, it is that bad boss who will have proven a "good teacher," by showing you how *not* to treat your employees.

No matter how desperate you may be to move on, there's always *something* to be gained from where you are in the present. And if you don't figure out that something, two very damaging results can occur. First, when you fail to recognize the value of your current station, you can't help but put forth a substandard effort and feel miserable about what you're doing. It's almost impossible to feel motivated when all you can see is hopelessness and negativity. And second, in your efforts to find a new job, that deflated attitude may come across to prospective employers.

Introspection is always a very necessary part of a job search. And while it's easy to see a lot of external factors as the cause for your displeasure, if you don't stop to figure out the negatives you may be bringing to the table, you're bound to repeat the same mistakes in your next job.

How to Work It

I'll let you in on a secret. There's a trick to getting the most out of any job—and it's not what you think. Lots of folks insist that you must gain a sense of fulfillment, joy, and satisfaction from the work you do. I pooh-pooh that theory. You don't *have* to love your job. You don't even have to like it—though it helps. What you must do in any job in order to be successful is know how to make the most of it—right now. In other words, you need to know how to *work it.*

Now, to a lot of sisters that may sound like settling. I'm certainly not suggesting that. You can still suit up and look for better opportunities if you feel you need to, and you can still go back to school or develop new skills. In fact, you can have one foot already out the door. But in the meantime, don't *fight* your job. *Work* your job.

Look with objectivity at the job you have now. Are you getting the kind of recognition for your work that you deserve? If the answer is no, ask yourself this: Can you truly say you've explored all possible avenues for growth? Most sisters and brothers—especially bootstrappers—were taught to work, and work hard. We were not schooled, however, in the fine art of *working it*. Many of our parents and our parents' parents were laborers and menial workers who succeeded by dint of their strength and character. They were reliable, hardworking, and honest—and that was enough.

In this day and age, if you're naïve enough to believe that the promotions and plum assignments are fairly doled out to the noblest and most deserving employees, it's time to wake up and smell the caffe latte. You need to devote almost as much time and energy on mastering the politics as on doing the job itself. That's especially true if you aren't adept at subtle self-promotion maneuvers.

Get Ahead

If, like many a sister, you're plugging away at your job, arriving on time, doing all that is expected, and *waiting* for your promotion to come through, you've got a lot to learn. The first thing you have to do in order to get ahead is make sure you're more than a blip on your boss's radar screen. You have to get yourself noticed. And simply doing a good job is not the way to do that.

Now, we don't come from a culture where self-promotion is often rewarded. Quite the contrary. When somebody comes around talking about what they've got, what they've done, and what they're doing, we all know they get a reputation real fast. "Who the hell does she think she is?" our peers say. "She thinks she's cute." The list of put-downs goes on and on.

But unless you want to wither and die in the secretarial pool, you're going to have to forget some of the rules your mama taught you. What is regarded as polite and respectful in our black social or church circles is often useless and downright foolish in the workplace. I'm not suggesting you lose your identity or "Tom" your way up the ladder. But you've got to make sure you are not some nameless face in the crowd of workers to whom your boss gives a simple nod of acknowledgment and keeps on stepping.

Self-promotion doesn't have to be shameless. Try a few of these simple hints to boost your office profile.

Ten Ways to Get Ahead

✦ **PUT IT IN A MEMO.** Toot your own horn in writing. Unless you bring your accomplishments to your boss's attention, many of your best skills—like the ability to organize, manage, and execute—may go unnoticed. There are myriad opportunities to do this. The key is timing. For example, at the end of any successful project, write up a brief summary of events—lauding the work of others, but particularly highlighting *your* contributions. Another keen memo opportunity? In the midst of a difficult project, apprise your boss of the challenges and potential glitches—again with special emphasis on what you're doing to maintain control. This tack serves a dual purpose: Bosses hate surprises. If and when something goes wrong, she'll appreciate the fact that you kept her in the loop.

✦ **CURRY FAVOR.** Without getting too chummy, make it your business to know and appreciate your boss's likes and dislikes. And do favors—of a professional nature—for him or her. For example, do extra work whenever possible and volunteer for tough assignments.

✦ **SHOW YOU GIVE A DAMN.** Volunteering for charity work outside the office or initiating some charitable move inside the office is an ideal way to do good and get your name out at the same time. Donate your efforts to any cause you care about and promote the issue as much as you can. If there is a company newsletter, try to use it to gain coverage. Note: Remember, in this case, you *do* want to keep emphasis on the cause and not on you or your involvement. There is a fine line—but don't cross it.

✦ **TALK THE TALK.** Professional talk, that is. No matter how you speak at home or with your girls, when you're at the job you must speak as well as you know how. *Black Enterprise* magazine's Earl Graves once said, "The global economy does not trade in black English." No matter how qualified you are, the use of improper grammar can do your professional image irreparable harm and only plays into the dozens of black stereotypes we face on the job. It's sad to say, but an African-American who is well-spoken is truly a novelty to most whites.

✦ **SIDE STEP.** Don't be afraid to make lateral moves. Too often we may look at a move within the company only in terms of increased pay or lofty title. A willingness to make strategic lateral moves demonstrates to employers that you are adaptable—a very important trait of skilled managers. Moreover, this is a good way to gain experience. The more skills you have, the more valuable you are to an employer.

✦ **PUT ON A HAPPY FACE.** You don't have to go around grinning like a Cheshire cat. But *do* keep a lid on the negative vibes. Don't complain out loud (you never know who's listening).

And in an environment where most everyone feels over-worked, your positive attitude will make you a standout among your peers. It's especially important to keep your spirits up when the pressure is on. This is not to say you won't ever have legitimate reasons to gripe. Everyone gets frustrated; just try not to let it show.

✦ **MAKE YOUR BOSS YOUR COUNSEL.** Be sure to talk to your boss about your goals and seek her advice early and often. If it looks as though you're content in your current post, your name will never come to mind when there's an opportunity for advancement. When you're aware that there's an opening at a higher level, let it be known that you'd like to be considered for it. Ambition is a good thing, as long as you're not cut-throat about it.

✦ **KEEP A RECORD.** Keep notes of the beyond-the-call-of-duty things you do. These are the small and large things that in and of themselves may not get much attention. Don't assume that your boss is aware of the late hours and weekends you put in. And you don't want to flood him with memos and paperwork. Keeping your own records will come in handy when you want to lobby for a raise or promotion. With notes, you'll be able to speak in specifics and make pointed references to your contributions, rather than deal in generalities like "I work really hard."

✦ **GET IN ON THE ACTION.** If you want to be noticed, you've got to be in the game, not benched on the sidelines. Take a look at where the company is putting its resources and betting on growth. That's where you want to be. This, of course, requires that you constantly stay on top of your game. Just imagine, for example, if you'd been Internet savvy when your firm was making a push toward e-commerce.

✦ **DRESS WELL.** I purposely ranked this last, although most professional advice regarding on-the-job success gives it higher billing. Most of us are already aware of the power of clothes. If anything, I think we sometimes emphasize style to a fault. Being well dressed, professionally speaking, is not a matter of being turned out in the latest runway styles. Unless you work in fashion, I'd advise keeping designer logos and labels hidden from view. If you're outdressing your boss, you may risk alienating her. That doesn't mean she's a hater; it's just that your heightened focus on fashion can imply a lack of seriousness. Instead, shift your attention to the subtleties of fine dressing: Keep your shoes polished and in good repair, keep an extra pair of hose on hand in case of runs, and don't let things like missing buttons and ragged hemlines wreck your look.

It's a Sistah Thang

If you've read up to this point, then you obviously believe as I do: There's nothing like being a sister. We're survivors. We're soulful. We're strong. We're stylish. And, most of the time, we're pretty sure of ourselves. In the workplace, however, all those fine qualities sometimes seem to work against us. They often cause us to be misguided, mistreated, and—at best—plain old misunderstood. When we enter the corporate world speaking boldly, poised, and well dressed, we come across as very confident. Whether we are or not isn't the point; we're viewed that way. And for some, that can be a bit disarming. When we wear our hair in locks or twists, we baffle many who don't share our cultural heritage. Not necessarily because they're racist, but because they're simply confounded by our large array of hairstyles and textures. What do "locks" mean, they wonder? Is she militant? How is it that she had long braids last week and a shoulder-length bob today?

The truth is, on both sides we suffer from vast and enduring perception problems from jump street. The way we usually express ourselves runs counter to the way many of our white counterparts were brought up to express themselves. They tend to be understated and self-effacing. We are apt to be bold and outspoken, and, yes, sometimes hands get placed squarely on hips, index fingers point, and necks roll.

In heated discussions we are seen as quite intimidating. Our eyes fix; our voices rise. There is little holding back. By contrast, many white women are brought up to avoid conflict altogether. They often tiptoe into a controversy and, with shaky but smiling faces, wait for the aggressor to begin. Then they articulate their words very gingerly. In fact, if you notice, in the mouths of many white women, potentially prickly statements manage to come out in the form of a question. For example, a black woman might say, "You really need to speak to me with respect." A white woman voicing the same sentiment might say, "I'm kind of concerned about the way you sometimes speak to me? I'm sensing some hostility?" I offer this insight only to highlight the cultural chasm that sometimes gapes between us.

So where does that leave the humble, bootstrapping sister striving to make it? Do we set out to educate the unenlightened and make ourselves present-day missionary zealots? Do we focus our every waking moment on trying to be understood, like ambassadors of blackness? No, of course not. Even if we desired to take on such a crusade, it would be fruitless. I've seen many a sister become so preoccupied with proving that she's different from the perceived notions that she completely loses herself in the process.

What we must do is much simpler: We must become more aware of our own behavior. We must learn that there are ways to maintain our identities yet foster communication without inciting fear or intimidation. If that sounds like kowtowing to you, think about it this way. If you were talking to a fidgety two-year-old, you wouldn't curse out the little tyke because he knocked over a glass figurine, would you? No, you would recognize, no matter how disappointed you might be to lose your prized objet d'art, that he didn't mean to do it.

I'm not putting white corporate America on par with nursery school. But what I'm saying is that, with the exception of overtly racist or sexist incidents, most offenses occur out of ignorance. So rather than respond with anger, defuse such situations with a degree of class and professionalism. If you find it too difficult to maintain your composure, take a moment—count to ten, go to the ladies' room, or just pray. Then address the situation calmly.

Winning Words

What you say and how you say it are crucial to your success in a professional environment. Your objective is to come across as a team player at all times. You won't have a ready answer for every situation that comes up, but you should show a willingness to help troubleshoot when you can. Rather than say "I don't know," try "I'll get back to you on that." Then be certain to follow up in a timely fashion.

Choose your words with care, no matter whom you're talking to. It's important to realize that your boss is not the only person you want to impress. Getting the most out of any job means forming alliances with everyone you can. Speak with everyone—from the CEO to the folks in the mailroom—with the same degree of respect and sincerity. Not just because it's the right thing to do but also because you never know when you'll need that secretary or that messenger to get *your* job done effectively. The old saying "what goes around comes around" was never more applicable than in a workplace environment. Assistants rotate throughout departments. Responsibilities are often juggled. You just never know . . .

We're all very busy, and most of us tend to think that almost no one is *as* busy as we. So it's sometimes easy to "blow someone off" in the name of prioritizing. Check yourself; employers look to promote people who are not only good at what they do but who know how to work well with others—and that includes communicating in a productive and positive way.

Do you know the power of winning words? Take the quiz below and see how you rank.

1. Someone on your team asks, "What's the status of the Jones file?" You have no idea. You respond: (a) "I couldn't tell you." (b) "I'll follow up with marketing." (c) "Missy had it last, not me."

2. It's past seven o'clock on a Friday evening, and after a long day, you're ready to go home. A vice president to whom you do not report asks your help in finishing up a project. You say: (a) "Do you know what time it is? I'm outta here." (b) "I wouldn't be any good to you at this point. How about if I come in early on Monday?" (c) "Don't you have an assistant?"

3. You've been working on an important assignment, and the deadline is fast approaching. Someone from the mailroom comes by selling candy for his church. You say: (a) "I'm busy; come back later." (b) "You bet; I'll stop by this afternoon with the money." (c) "See my secretary; she'll take care of you."

4. Your boss is hosting a group from the company's home office. You're in the middle of a marketing plan he asked you to do this morning when he requests that you show some of them around. You say: (a) "How can I? You've got me doing . . ." (b) "If you don't mind my putting the marketing plan aside, I'd

76

be glad to." (c) "Sure, I can finish this old marketing plan anytime."

5. You're making a big presentation and wearing your best designer suit—a four-hundred-dollar number from Saks. In the ladies' room, one of the secretaries admiringly asks you where you bought it. You suddenly feel self-conscious, because you believe she couldn't afford it. You say: (a) "Girl, this thing probably costs as much as your rent." (b) "I got it at Saks, a special treat for myself." (c) "Uh, I can't remember."

Key: If you answered (a) the vast majority of the time, you could use a few lessons in tact. Remember, complete honesty is *not* always the best policy. More (b) answers indicate that you at least know how to come off as a consensus builder by choosing winning words. A lot of (c) responses mean you're a pro when it comes to passing the buck. You're the polar opposite of a team player.

When in Rome . . .

What I did at Roy Rogers—wear my uniform with pride, speak in a friendly Western drawl, and take on cheerleaderlike enthusiasm—was what I needed to do to in order to succeed in that environment. I didn't go in and try to shake up the place. They'd been selling fast food for many years before I came along and would continue doing so long after my departure. They had their own—albeit hokey—formula, and it worked.

How far you excel on the job depends greatly on how well you play by the rules—not only the formal ones found in your employee manual but also the unwritten codes of conduct that seep into the environment. I've made a point to do just that in every position I've ever held. And if you don't want to knock your head against a brick wall and be relegated to dead-end status within a company, you have to do the same. As quickly as possible, figure out the landscape of the playing field and learn to play the game.

On the surface it may appear as though corporate America is corporate America no matter where you are: a bunch of old white men in suits, handing dictates down to the rest of us. There are, of course, the obvious rules and standards of professional behavior. But while there are certainly similarities among professional environments, it will serve you well to understand the nuances. Usually you can't waltz into a bank or law firm wearing tight jeans and a halter top, for example. And you may be expected to address everyone by last names. On the other hand, if you worked for a hip-hop record company, that outfit might be totally acceptable, and nicknames might be the way to address everyone, including the boss. But even within like industries, there are sure to be differences.

And unfortunately, what you don't know *can* hurt you—even kill you, from a career standpoint. Just like people, companies have "personalities": Some are reserved, others more laid-back. You wouldn't approach someone you barely know with a dirty joke or details of your sex life, would you? No, you respect certain boundaries. Likewise, you should never get too familiar with your co-workers until you learn the culture or personality of your employer.

When you examine a company's culture, you cannot do so in a vacuum. As carefully as you review the personality of the chief executive and personnel, you must also look at your own. Not everybody can adapt to every kind of company. If you're a methodical person who thrives among established systems and hierarchical structures, you may chafe against the laid-back style of a young dot-com start-up. Where you may be accustomed to formally conducted meetings and countless memoranda, they may operate in an open-door, shoot-from-the-hip manner. Of course, you may learn to appreciate the different styles. But you should at least be aware that the potential for conflict is there, and you'll have to be flexible in order to make a good fit.

Whatever you do, don't sleep on the importance of working *with,* rather than against, the established culture of your workplace. And it doesn't matter where you work—a mom-and-pop shop or a Fortune 500 corporation—each and every employer has one. Corporate culture, just like the culture of a people, can be difficult to articulate fully. But that doesn't mean it doesn't exist. Think about our own sister circle. If you cock your head to one side and narrow your gaze, there is probably not an African-American person in North America who can't decipher that body language; it's a part of our culture. You need to be able to understand the unspoken words of your workplace just as well. Here are a few guidelines to help you break the code—dress and otherwise.

+ **DRESS CODE.** This is one of the most obvious indications of an employer's personality. But don't be fooled—it is not a determinant in and of itself. In the past few years almost every workplace has loosened the restrictive, buttoned-up dress codes of past eras. Even traditionally staid corporations like IBM have adopted business-casual dress policies. Usually, though not always, "relaxed" dress codes are the sign of a somewhat informal corporate culture.

+ **AGE.** To a certain extent, the age of a company and its senior management staff can influence the direction of the company culture. Younger firms may tend to be less hierarchical and more entrepreneurial than their more mature counterparts. Conversely, a venerable industry leader may be more tradition-bound and formal.

+ **TECHNOLOGY.** The extent to which a firm embraces new technologies is, in many ways, an indication of how progressive and open its upper management may be to new ideas. Even if the company's core business is not related to high-tech, look at the emphasis (or lack thereof) it places on innovative advancements that could help increase productivity.

+ **SIZE.** Often, though not always, a company's size may tell you how procedural it is. For example, a large company is likely to rely more on written communiqués than is a smaller organization, which is probably less formal.

There may be times when you totally misread a company's culture. You may go in for an interview, even take a walk around the place, and have one impression—only to discover that the opposite is the case. That's why it is so important when starting a new position that you devote the first few weeks to careful observation. Sit back and take in your surroundings before trying to change things or announce bold ideas.

On some level I know most of this culture talk seems obvious. But trust me, sister, the most sophisticated folks—and even multinational corporations—can be led astray. Take the case of Snapple, the quirky iced-tea and beverage maker. By the early nineties this company had grown into a multimillion-dollar concern and captured the attention of several of its larger competitors, including Quaker Oats, the maker of Gatorade, among other products. Quaker acquired Snapple, and almost from day one the union proved disastrous. The entreprenurial mind-set of Snapple and its workers couldn't seem to gel with its far more staid and corporate partner. Only a few years later, Quaker Oats unloaded Snapple, losing millions of dollars and much credibility on Wall Street in the process.

Office Politics: Play or Get Played

Once you feel comfortable with the lay of the land, you're far from home free. You can't win or succeed on the job until you learn to play the game. It matters little whether you work for a small or large company, whether the company is mature and sober or young and trendy—no organization is without its share of politics, the mind games and subtle strategies that become like the governing communications dialect of a workplace. And it's crucial, too, that you are conversant in the lingo, because it often becomes a kind of office shorthand for getting a point across and maintaining good relationships with your boss and co-workers.

For example, every organization has a power circle of influence. You are most likely aware—or at least you should be—of your firm's chain of command. This is different. The power circle is made up of those folks who have the boss's ear, the folks for whom her door is always open. No appointment necessary. It is sometimes not enough to please your boss. Often the name of this game is first forming an alliance with members of this inner circle. Unfortunately, there are as many sides to office politics as there are employers, so it's impossible to list them all.

Just understand that office politics are a natural outgrowth of a corporate culture or personality. There are, of course, some broad brushstrokes, but the full picture comes across in the subtle shadings. To bring it home, if you've ever spent time with your man's family, you've probably experienced that striking moment when you realize his people are not like yours. Maybe they are a boisterous and outspoken lot, while your family is more reserved. These kinds of differences are not usually such a big problem; with both sides working together, most of us learn how to decode each other's communicating styles and get along.

As sisters in the corporate world, however, we often feel as though we are at a distinct disadvantage. That's because the office shorthand is usually native to the dominant or ruling body—read: white males. The first step toward cracking the established politics at your job is becoming aware that it exists and how it affects you. Without this understanding, you risk getting played by a system you may feel powerless to overcome.

As black women in corporate settings, we are played more often than we may know. While our brothers are usually hit over the head with obvious signs of hostility, we can easily be lulled into complacency. We are viewed as far less threatening, far less angry, thus far "safer" than black men. There are some whites who feel an almost instant affinity for us. Perhaps they were reared by a warm and loving black nanny. Or maybe they are drawn to the overt sexual images perpetuated by the media à la some of our supermodels and other sexy stars. In any case, on the surface, we might feel accepted.

But don't be fooled. Sometimes you may have to go beyond the smiles and glad-handing of some to see a pattern of disparity. There are a few palpable clues that you may be misplaying your hand in the game of office politics. To keep from getting caught up in a veritable firestorm, make it your business to know the signs.

✦ "SUPERWOMAN." Because of your diligence and hard work, you are the go-to person on many key accounts or projects. And over the course of your tenure, you have seen a steady increase in your responsibilities. Yet when promotion time rolls around, you're overlooked.

✦ "HELLO? CAN YOU HEAR ME?" You open the meeting with a great idea for the company's latest product. It is met with a patronizing "Nice thought" or some such. Moments later a white male counterpart has distilled your thought as though it were his own. Wrapped in jargon and fancy office-speak, "his" idea is proclaimed as "bold" and "outside the box." And by the meeting's end he is hailed as the best thing since sliced bread.

✦ "IS IT ME?" You find that you're out of the loop when it comes to some of the company's social events. Sure, you get the major announcements like the Christmas party e-mail. But because you don't participate in Monday-morning water cooler talk about your weekend fairway escapades, no one bothers to tell you about the charity golf tournament, which just happens to draw all of the firm's regional higher-ups. As discouraging as such scenarios may appear, don't dismay. In and of themselves, they do not spell the end of a promising career. All they do is present momentary challenges. And they're not as difficult to overcome as you may think.

Get Your Game On

A professional sister-friend of mine often tells the story of how, in sheer frustration with the politics within the sales company she worked for, she turned to her mother—a simple, churchgoing woman who worked as a domestic most of her life. Her mother listened patiently as her daughter complained about the "games of white folk." And after she'd finished venting, her mother looked at her and said, "It sounds rough, baby. But that's why they call it *work*. I never heard nobody say they was going to play."

Of course, girlfriend had to laugh at the raw wisdom of her mother's statement. She realized that, like anything, winning at office politics required work. Once she accepted that very simple fact, her on-the-job interactions went much more smoothly. She didn't have to lose her identity or pretend to be someone other than herself. She merely had to recognize that this "game" required tapping into a new set of skills—some of which she already owned, but had lain dormant.

For example, she would never have let a slight go unchecked in her social circle. Yet, instead of confronting her superiors on the job, she would retreat to her girls or her mother and complain to them. Usually the conversation would begin, "You won't believe what those people on the job are trying to do to me . . ." And the whine session was on.

No more, she vowed. Instead, she would take her issues straight to the source without letting them fester. Often she found that gentle confrontation alone was enough to squelch the offense. Other strategies include the following:

+ **CUT 'EM SOME SLACK.** No one can deny it; we live in a sexist, racist, and elitist society. But that doesn't mean that discrimination is always at the root of a problem. Most of what seems unjust treatment comes from a place of ignorance or benign neglect, not from a place of maliciousness. If a conflict arises, don't automatically make your race and gender the focal point; keep it in perspective.

+ **BE IN IT TO WIN IT.** You don't have to grin all day if that's not your style. But as sisters in a white male world, we can ill afford to be perceived as angry or exclusionary. Otherwise you risk alienating your peers as well as the decision makers responsible for your rise. Make some effort to be friendly, and even if you don't enjoy some of the same things—like golf, for example—demonstrate some willingness to learn.

+ **EXERCISE YOUR FUNNY BONE.** Sometimes the best way to handle a slight is with humor. For example, if someone steals your idea in a meeting, rather than fume silently you might say something like "Gee, I'm glad to see great minds think alike. That's exactly the proposal I made ten minutes ago!"

Your quick-witted response serves two purposes: You're asserting yourself and showing you can be graceful under fire.

✦ **MENTORING MATTERS.** Identify someone in your field, although not necessarily in your company, who is seasoned and savvy. Just like friendships, mentor relationships grow over time and have to gel on both sides. Look for someone whose style you admire, be up-front about your career goals and challenges, then slowly cultivate a relationship. Remember that there should be something in it for both parties. Maybe the mentor will score points of her own by cultivating your growth. Increasing cultural diversity is the charge for many corporations, and those who do so are often rewarded. Perhaps, for your part, you can simply help the busy executive by occasionally offering to run errands.

✦ **NETWORK, NETWORK, NETWORK.** This is key if you want to thrive in your chosen profession. The advantages are manifold. Professional organizations and other networking outlets can help raise your profile and your morale, boosting your chances for promotions in your current job. You develop your communications skills and enhance your assertiveness. And finally, your heightened profile increases your chances of getting a better job in the event you choose to jump ship.

✦ **TAKE IT HIGHER.** Before you let anger and frustration take you over and sabotage your chances for advancement, speak to your superior about your concerns. If that doesn't work, talk to *his* boss—but only as a last resort and only if you're prepared to deal with the possible fallout that may result. Rather than saying simply, "I'm not treated fairly," point to specific incidents and have documentation to back up your assertions.

✦ **HANG IN THERE.** Sometimes what's needed are strength and perseverance. Don't give up just because the going gets tough.

You can fight the good fight by sticking to your principles and being assertive but not in-your-face aggressive. One of television's highest-ranking sisters, Paula Walker Madison, was named vice president and news director of WNBC in New York only after she toiled for years as the station's number-two executive. She even saw a male colleague promoted ahead of her before she finally landed the job. Her fortitude paid off big time. Just this year, she was tapped as president and general manager of KNBC in Los Angeles.

Boss Appeal

Boss appeal is much like sex appeal. When people truly have it, there is an aura about them that's hard for anyone to resist. They're confident, yet not cocky. They're smart, but never condescending. They seem to possess just the right blend of levity that draws their co-workers to them and the seriousness that wins their employers' respect. In short, those with boss appeal are a pleasure to work with.

They have that indescribable, intangible quality that separates the office drones from the superstars. Face it. No one wants to be a brown-noser, lose all self-respect, and earn the scorn of co-workers. But there are few of us who don't want to be the boss's pet. That's the sister who gets heaped with undying praise in memo after memo, the one who can always seem to get prized face time with the head honcho, and—you guessed it—the sister most likely to succeed.

But what happens when you become the exact opposite of the boss's favorite and instead find yourself the object of her wrath? No matter what you do, there seems to be no pleasing her. She somehow manages to ruin your day with a single criticism and just generally make your nine-to-five life a living hell. That's when you need Difficult Boss Management 101.

You don't have to like your boss, but you must show him or her respect. Too often, what many of us do is let a personality clash come between us and our success at work. We turn a difficult boss into our archenemy. We make the professional conflict personal and lose our cool. Or we forget that life is not necessarily fair and we succumb to the role of victim ("My boss hates me, so . . ."). In truth, there are very few bosses, even the raging tyrannical ones, who cannot be tamed—or at least managed. It takes patience. It takes objectivity. But most of all it takes self-control. A difficult supervisor does not *have* to drive you away from your job.

Before you bolt, consider these steps:

Boss Control

+ **ACCENTUATE THE POSITIVE.** Bosses are just regular folk with power. Yes, your boss may have a short temper, but is she a decent and ultimately a fair person overall? Then don't take the outbursts to heart. And don't let one or two shortcomings paint the entire picture.

+ **NOTE WHAT TRIGGERS THE BEHAVIOR.** Although there are exceptions, not that many people fly off the handle for no reason whatsoever. What is your boss's breaking point? What sets him off? Tardiness? Sloppy work? Identify the catalyst to his behavior, then act accordingly.

+ **DECIDE IF IT'S PERSONAL.** Is it you, or is the guy a monster to any- and everyone? If it's the latter, don't take the behavior personally or go out of your way to antagonize him.

+ **SPEAK UP.** If the situation is out of hand, arrange a face-to-face meeting with your boss, stressing that you show her respect and expect the same in return. Keep your temper in check and cite specific injustices, rather than just whining something like "Why are you so mean to me?" Sometimes this kind of simple tête-à-tête is enough to put a stop to the behavior. Some bullies pipe down once they are confronted.

✦ **KNOW WHEN TO SAY WHEN.** If every reasonable approach fails, you might want to transfer out of the department or look to change jobs. If such is the case, you must be careful never to give in to the temptation to talk about the personality clash with your boss. Even if your reasons are valid, you risk looking like a whiner or—even worse—someone who can't get along with others.

Stressing It

We all know what it *feels* like to be stressed out by work. But what exactly *is* stress? Is there a way to avoid it? Or are we all doomed in this high-speed Information Age of the twenty-first century to feel besieged from all sides? Believe it or not, there isn't a person alive who doesn't experience stress. You might fantasize at times about moving to some island paradise where you loll around all day and feed off the fruits of the earth. But you know what? There would still be stresses. What happens if there's a hurricane and your crops founder?

Stress is not defined by a particular lifestyle. Stress is that physical and mental tension we experience when we face a tough situation—and it's different for everybody. To some degree we all live with stress daily. And, in and of itself, stress is a good thing. Do you think Venus Williams was stress-free when she captured her Wimbledon title? And don't you feel a certain level of stress when you're caught up in a passionate kiss?

It's part of the human condition, see? Whenever our brains sense danger or even excitement—whether real or imagined—a physical reaction is set in motion. Chemicals in the body are activated that in no uncertain terms tell the nervous system, "You're in danger, girl." With that, your body shifts into high gear.

Imagine you're that caveperson, staring into the vicious eyes of a saber-toothed tiger (stress is *that* old). Your heartbeat quickens. And as the beast licks his chops, something called a "fight or flight" response kicks in. In other words, you have two choices: You can try fighting off the tiger with your bare hands (probably not a good idea) or you can run like you stole something. This primal sequence of events takes place every time we encounter challenges.

Now that you know how stress works in the body, the next step is to figure out how stress is affecting you in your own life. For many of us, our jobs and professional lives are the largest source of stress. That's no surprise, given that most Americans are working longer and harder than ever before. It matters little whether you're a white- or a blue-collar worker—senior management, midlevel, or clerical—we're all responsible for something at our jobs.

See if you agree with any of the following to determine whether you are a candidate for work-related stress:

A. I'm under pressure to perform.

B. I feel I have little control over my work process.

C. I'm in a position of responsibility.

If any of the above apply to your situation you probably feel stressed at work. But you're hardly alone. A Gallup poll found that 90 percent of us feel stressed at work. The Department of Health and Human Services reports that stress costs American industry more than $300 billion each year in absenteeism, reduced productivity, and Worker's Compensation benefits. That's $7,500 for each employee annually. In 1991 *The New England Journal of Medicine* reported a connection between stress and the common cold. In the study, subjects were exposed to a cold virus through nasal spray. Those who were under stress (determined by a questionnaire) were more than twice as likely to catch a cold as those who were not under stress. Since then, research has shown that between 80 and 90 percent of all illness is stress-related.

Top Ten Signs of Stress

+ Insomnia

+ Persistent fatigue

+ Nail biting

+ Irritability

+ Intestinal disorders

+ Lack of concentration

+ Hunger for sweets

+ Rapid pulse rate

+ Frequent illness, including headaches and colds

+ Lower-back or other muscle pain

Which of these scenarios do you think would be universally defined as stressful?

A. Making a presentation to your company's board of directors

B. Spending over an hour at the Department of Motor Vehicles

C. The death of a loved one

You may be wondering why "all of the above" is not given as an option here. Surely each of these hypothetical situations could be distressing. But the fact is, only the death of a loved one is something that would *definitely* cause stress. The other external events depend largely on your point of view. A chance to present yourself before a body of heavyweight decision makers could be an exciting opportunity to shine. A slow-moving bureaucracy doesn't have the power to stress you out unless you choose to let it.

Think of stress as the Baskin-Robbins of human emotions—"31-derful" flavors and growing. In other words, there are as many varieties of stress as there are people. There's the anxiety you might feel on a typical weekday morning when you're running late for your eight-thirty meeting, your kids have missed the bus and a pileup has brought traffic to a standstill. There's the trauma of dealing with cataclysmic change, such as the death of a loved one—and there's everything in between. But when you get right down to it, most of the stress in our lives is self-induced.

In other words, being cut off by a rude driver during your morning commute is not necessarily stressful in and of itself. It only becomes so when we choose to elevate the slight and begin consuming ourselves with revenge schemes for the next several miles. The more attuned we become to *what* stresses us and effective ways of dealing with stress, the more we can control the way stress affects our lives. During the average workday many things can "get to you," but some stresses are more common than others.

What's Eating You?

If you don't beat down your stresses, they'll beat you. To get your arms around the things that stress you out, you'll need to find a system of recognizing your stress and then figuring out how to reduce it. There are three basic steps involved in this process:

1. **SEE IT.** Get in touch with the things that stress you out and know them like the back of your hand. How does it look? Where does it come from? Maybe it's deadline pressures at work. Maybe it's a lack of resources—tools or support staff—you need to do your job well.

2. **KNOW IT.** Think about the way you usually deal with this stress and then determine some alternative ways of coping. If you typically yell or seethe inside, your answer could be as simple as addressing your concerns in a memo or meeting with your boss. But you may need to change the situation or change yourself. That is, change jobs or put your stress in perspective.

3. **DO IT.** Act on the stress to reduce its effects. This could mean taking up relaxation exercises, managing your time better, or delegating more effectively.

One of the surest ways to get stressed out at work is to bite off more than you can chew. If your "in" box is toppling onto the floor, there's a good chance you're not organizing your time efficiently. Some of us are loath to let on that our workloads are getting the best of us, so we take on more and more tasks. Many of us fear that our supervisors will think less of us if we decline an assignment. In fact, quite the opposite is true. Any manager worth her salt wants a job done well and will appreciate your forthrightness if you admit you can't do a project justice. Simply say something like "Which of the projects I'm working on already can I put on the back burner to get this one done?" Or "I'm juggling four assignments right now. Which one should be my priority?"

Stress Busters

If you're not the parent of a young child, I suggest you borrow one for the next exercise. Imagine a two-year-old who stayed up past his bedtime last night, fought against his noontime nap, and has now climbed into the cookie jar. What do you have? A tired, cranky kid on a maddening sugar high whose erratic moods find him bawling one moment, dancing the next, and kicking and screaming his way into tantrum-filled misery. It's not pretty.

But unfortunately, it's not a far cry from the way some of us adults treat our own bodies. Waking groggy-eyed from an evening of late-night TV, we push ourselves through the day with a string of quick fixes, including caffeine, sugar, and greasy snacks. Then we wonder why we're cranky and ill at ease.

There is a better way. We can reduce the level of stress in our lives dramatically by making smarter lifestyle choices. That means eating nutritiously, exercising regularly, and practicing relaxation techniques. Ideally, aim to meditate in the morning and at night. But if you're in a stressful situation and meditation is not an option, try some deep-breathing exercises.

✦ Inhale very slowly through your nose, expanding your abdomen.

✦ Slowly exhale through your mouth, pulling in your abdominal muscles and releasing all the air from your lungs.

✦ Continue these two steps until you establish a natural rhythm.

Calling It Quits

There comes a time in just about any job when you realize that, for whatever reason, you've gone as far as you can go. It's important to recognize this point—the sooner the better. Some of us wait until we're utterly sick and tired of a place, and then we begin to act out, caught up in a cycle of negativity and frustration.

Each situation is different, and only you can determine what's best for you and your career goals. But if you're waffling—unsure whether you're experiencing a natural phase of boredom or truly ready to jet—examine the following.

It's time to clock out when:

+ The number of others ahead of you make promotion prospects dim. Or maybe it's a family business and you've risen as far as you can expect to.

+ You're bored to tears. There's no such thing as the perfect job, but if you're about to lose your mind, it may be time to move on. Before you do, though, make an honest assessment of the present situation. Can you get more responsibilities, transfer internally?

+ You're locked into a cycle of being overworked and underpaid, with little chance of change.

+ Your workload is steadily increasing, but your paycheck remains the same. There are times when a good worker is given lots more work with no compensation because she doesn't complain or make her wants and needs known. Talk to your boss about money, and if that doesn't work, moving on may be the answer.

✦ You've been passed over for a promotion (again). Think long and hard. If you can be objective and see that you were the most logical person and lost out, you may not have a future here.

✦ Your gut tells you so; there's no logical reason. Listen to your heart. You must honor your own emotional instincts.

Chapter 5

FINANCIAL FREEDOM

$\mathcal{M}$y parents always made sure to shelter us kids from any financial hardships they may have been facing. The only clue I had that it was sometimes tough making ends meet was when my mother would call home from work asking if the mailman had come yet. If I told her yes, she instructed me to immediately place the mail in the hallway credenza, before my father got home. Though she said no more, I knew what that meant. There were bills in that day's delivery, bills we didn't have the money to pay. Rather than see her husband upset or frustrated, my mother chose to conceal those bills for as long as possible, in hopes that before long she'd be able to reconcile our meager means with the utility companies, mortgage lender, and insurance agent. Somehow she usually did.

In our household there was no sophisticated system for managing money. I believe that my parents had a checking account, where they kept just enough money to cover the checks they wrote out for bills. But a savings account? I have vivid memories of my dad literally stowing any extra money underneath their mattress for safekeeping. There was no interest-bearing savings account and certainly no investment portfolio.

Growing up as I did, with my parents living paycheck to paycheck, informed my choices in many ways. It's hard to miss that which you've never had, so I've been totally unimpressed by the trappings of material wealth for as long as I can remember. In fact, I can even remember being somewhat distrustful of people who had money and fancy things.

Still, I always knew that as an adult I would do my level best to make sure I was in a secure place with money. I didn't want to have to scrape, beg, or borrow—or hide bills from my partner. From the time I graduated from Howard in 1981 and moved out of my parents' home headed for the big city, I was watchful of my money. I rented a studio apartment in Manhattan's Chelsea area and shared it with my high-school friend Jackie. It was cramped, and while I probably could have stretched to make my starting reporter's salary of $13,000 a year cover the $650-a-month rent, by splitting the rent with Jackie, I would be able to save a little toward my dream of buying a house. I'd never lived in an apartment, and being a real grown-up to me meant having a place you owned, backyard and all.

Fortunately, I hadn't accumulated any debt while in college. Scholarships paid for the tuition, and my parents and I decided that I would simply live at home rather than shoulder the cost of campus living. Back then I was very much into clothes, and I had worked part-time jobs since the age of thirteen to finance my passion for fashion. Many of my friends, however, got caught up in the credit-card trap that's set especially for college students. I'd been raised to believe that if you didn't have the cash to pay for it, whatever it was, you weren't supposed to have it. While this kept me out of debt, it also kept me from establishing credit. So when I went to buy a car a year after moving to New York, it was no easy feat. I had moved to the borough of Brooklyn by then, and when I worked late nights, which was often, the company would pay for me to get a cab home. The problem was, I couldn't *get* a cab. It was the black thing combined with the fact that cabbies felt they would lose money because they'd have to drive back across the bridge to Manhattan with no fare.

After many arguments with taxi drivers, which often still resulted in me being left at the curb, I said, "That's it. I'm getting a car." So on a visit to D.C., my mom and I went to a Toyota dealership. When they ran a credit check, they discovered I had no credit. "That's right," I said smugly. "I don't owe anybody anything." Then the car salesman explained. You have to have established *some* credit in order to show that you can borrow money responsibly—that you do, in fact, pay your bills on time. Then he turned to my mother. "What about you? Can you cosign for her?" My mother looked nervous. Turns out that she once had had a credit card from Sears and had missed several payments. I ended up buying that car on my own—but at an interest rate of 18 percent! Right after that I signed up for two credit cards and used them sparingly, while paying them off in full each month religiously.

This practice served me well when I needed to demonstrate good credit to accomplish my goal of buying a house by age thirty, not an easy thing to do in pricey New York. I was about a year away from this milestone birthday when I met Glenn. Having him in my life made the goal more attainable because we could split the mortgage payments. We lived on two floors of the two-family house and rented out the top-floor apartment. The tenant's rent covered half the mortgage each month, and the part we paid was actually less than what each of us had been paying in rent for two separate apartments. We could have afforded to live in the entire house but chose not to so we could start to build a nest egg.

By the next year we had enough money saved to jump on a good deal for a brownstone around the corner. It was the first in five investment properties we've been able to acquire over the last ten years. Once we purchased one property, we used the equity built up in it to purchase the next. Even without the financial savvy of a Harvard M.B.A., I knew that real estate would allow me to accumulate wealth in a way that designer clothes and handbags never could.

True to bootstrapper form, we continue to live beneath our means. We buy used cars (few things depreciate faster than a new car driving off the lot). We buy items wholesale whenever possible. Groceries are bought at warehouse clubs, clothing at sample sales, outlet malls, and on clearance. To my mind there is nothing confining or sacrificing about this somewhat frugal lifestyle. I'm not materialistic, so doing without—especially in order to reach a long-term goal—has never pained me. Fortunately, my husband is the same way. And because of the example we've set, so is our nine-year-old daughter. Any windfall we receive—be it from our businesses, the stock market, or a raise in pay—is invested, either into an expansion venture or into a savings plan.

This is not to say, however, that we don't face financial challenges. Quite the contrary. Perhaps, due in equal parts to my bootstrapper mentality and Strong Black Woman tendencies, as I write this, we are facing the greatest financial risks of our lives. The renovation of our latest acquisition is running behind schedule and over budget, racking up weekly costs of nearly $5,000. In a race against the clock, we are desperately trying to launch our new coffeehouse, remodel six apartments, and build out space for two new retail tenants. Once all this is completed, we will be the proud owners of a thriving block-long urban "strip mall." But in the meantime, we're hedging our financial responsibilities like never before.

Because our accountant hasn't finished preparing our income tax return—it's complicated because it must reflect the financial statements of our businesses—we can't apply for bank loans. We've had to shoulder the cost of this project ourselves. That has meant drastic measures. Like my mother in her household, I'm the one who handles our family finances. And like her, too, I sometimes don't tell my husband just how tight things are, because his threshold for risk isn't quite as high as mine. Currently, to ensure a liquid cash-flow status for as long as possible, I'm paying our mortgages at the latest possible date without negatively affecting our credit—somewhere between the twenty-fifth and twenty-ninth of each month. After thirty days that's a blemish on your credit report, and it will stay there for at least seven years. We've maxed out all our credit cards, and I've also borrowed money from my 401(k) retirement plan. I'm in a race against the clock to return it within sixty days; otherwise I face a 10 percent penalty and have to pay income taxes on the loan. I'm juggling all of the family's discretionary spending like never before, carefully calculating the outlay for such "treats" as trips to the movies. Is it easy? Of course not. But I know that this, too, shall pass. In just a few months I know we will have a healthy revenue stream coming in from our newest investment.

Black Wealth—a Snapshot

If we as a community are ever to narrow the canyon-size disparity between the income and living standards of blacks and the rest of the population, we'll have to begin spending less and saving more. For far too long we've sought to enhance our standing in society by buying the symbols of status rather than achieving status. Given the fact that social respect has eluded African-Americans for so long, it might seem natural that we would take every opportunity to "flex" by acquiring the physical trappings of success—a fine car, fly clothes, so on. Whether on a conscious or subconscious level, it is as though we are trying to prove ourselves worthy of respect. "So what if we have to duck credit-card companies and other bill collectors to do it?" is our warped reasoning.

No doubt you have a sister-friend who is living in the fast lane. She earns an impressive salary, drives a late-model luxury car, dresses in the finest fashions—complete with signature accessories from the likes of Gucci, Fendi, and Louis—and jets off to a fabulous vacation getaway each year. Yet that same sister probably rents, rather than owns, her home. She has no assets to speak of, no substantial savings or retirement plan, and struggles to stay on top of a mountain of debt, including high-interest credit cards. Despite a comfortable salary, she lives a stressful paycheck-to-paycheck existence and has a negative net worth.

Unfortunately, there are many sisters like your girlfriend. The state of black wealth paints a dismal picture. As a people, we make up 12.7 percent of the United States population, earning 8 percent of the income. But we own merely 3 percent of the $2 trillion in assets held by American households. Yet, because of our aggressive spending habits, we are a powerfully attractive consumer market—with dozens and dozens of multinational consumer-product companies developing and targeting all kinds of goods and services to meet our needs and wants. *Target Market News,* a newsletter that tracks the spending habits of African-American consumers, reports that in 1996 we spent $422 million on panty-hose, $339 million on video rentals, and $410 million on CDs, records, and tapes. On average, we spent 25 percent more than our white counterparts did on color televisions. Yet we were 30 percent less likely to save money.

It's too easy to explain away this kind of wanton consumerism by saying that we owe ourselves such treats to compensate for the social hardships under which we endure. Let's go back. Madam C. J. Walker, one of my "sheroes," went from being a laundress to being a self-made millionaire—the first black woman in the U.S. to claim such an achievement. This was near the dawn of the twentieth century, a time when black suffering was at a dismal level. She created employment opportunities for thousands of fellow African-Americans. And at the same time that she built her own wealth, she contributed generously to the National Association for the Advancement of Colored People, Tuskegee University, and other organizations that served the greater interests of black folks.

Madam Walker lived large indeed, with a luxury mansion and lush estate on New York's scenic Hudson River. But she never did so at the expense of her future financial health. In 1914, when she spoke at the National Negro Business League, she told the audience, "I am preparing myself so that when this hair business falls to the ground, I will have an income."

How many of us are living by that example? Precious few, as statistics reveal:

+ The wealth gap between us and whites is as wide for blacks with earnings over $100,000 as it is for those who make under $25,000. In other words, even African-Americans with the means to get ahead are failing to do so.

+ By every measure we are less likely than whites to own substantial assets. In home ownership, for instance: 70 percent of whites owned their homes in 1995, while fewer than 50 percent of blacks were homeowners.

+ Blacks are a third less likely than whites to own stock.

+ Even though we make up about 13 percent of the population, blacks account for 54 percent of Americans who do not have checking accounts.

✦ While we are less likely to own assets, we are equally likely to carry debt. Both black and white families were burdened with a median debt of $10,000 in credit-card bills. But since our income is 40 percent less than whites', it takes us far longer to meet our debt obligations. This is particularly alarming given that blacks have only in recent decades won access to lines of credit, home loans, and other ways to run up debt.

✦ Our business ownership, another measure of wealth building, also lags that of whites in America, according to 1992 statistics, the latest figures available. The 620,912 black-owned enterprises constitute only 3.6 percent of all operating businesses in the United States. And a mere 3,000 of African-American-owned businesses reported annual revenue of more than a million dollars. Most (75 percent) took in less than $25,000 per year.

Money Messages

As black folks, we need to change our relationship with money—quick. We have to become friends with it, and believe that it's not only all right to have money but that it's *right* to have it. The sad truth is that many sisters (and brothers) don't truly believe they deserve prosperity. Some even believe it's somehow un-godly to desire an abundance of life's riches. Instead, they subscribe to the notion that virtue lies in poverty. The Reverend Floyd Flake, the popular New York City pastor and former congressman, has said that "heaven is not merely in the reward of the afterlife but in the heavenly environment that you create in this life," noting that biblical heroes such as Abraham and Solomon enjoyed great wealth. I say it's not the love of money that is the root of all evil; it's the lack of it that makes folk act crazy. A paucity of cash can wreak havoc or cloud our view in almost every aspect of our lives.

Who can ever forget the black woman's anthem of the eighties, "Ain't Nothin' Goin' On but the Rent"? Lines like "Ya gotta have a j-o-b to get wit' me" and "no romance without finance" became our mantras. More recently TLC warned us against "scrubs." Money can affect our relationships with men, leading us to stay with one or prompting us to ditch one, all based on what's in his pockets. It also heavily affects our career choices. Sometimes we stay in jobs that don't honor or fulfill us because we can't afford to miss a paycheck or we reason that "at least the job pays well." Financial insecurity limits our ability to make choices freely and control our own destiny.

Examine your relationship with money:

+ Do you spend more than you earn?

+ Do you record the checks you write and balance your checkbook?

+ If you were to stop working today, how long could you manage to stay afloat?

+ Do you carry credit-card balances from one month to another?

+ Do you treat or "pay" yourself back occasionally with personal gifts or rewards?

+ What portion of your income goes toward savings?

+ Do you run your finances, or do your finances run you?

Now, to really get in touch with your deepest and most visceral attitudes about money, review the messages you received about it as a child. If you grew up poor or if your parents did, they may have unwittingly left you a legacy of financial insecurity and feelings of lack. Think back to how your parents handled money and the messages you received from them.

+ Who controlled the money in your household? How did that person relate to money? Was he or she grateful for it or disgruntled because there was never enough? Throw it around freely or ration it spartanly?

+ As a child, did this person give you money generously? As reward for "good" behavior? In exchange for chores performed?

+ Did you feel rich or deprived as a child? Did you know how much your parents earned?

+ Were you expected to contribute to the household financially?

+ Looking back, what do you think you learned about money growing up, and how did it affect you?

Your answers to these questions about the past can help you come to a better understanding of how you regard money today. For example, I know of a sister who was raised on welfare by her single mom. Her mother felt bad about not being able to buy "luxuries" like fast-food meals and comic books. So when the first of the month rolled around, it was like Christmas at her house—the fridge was stocked; she and her siblings got new clothes and toys; the whole nine. Of course, it didn't take long before the family was broke. Today this sister-friend of mine is in her thirties and makes a comfortable fifty grand a year. Yet she tears through her salary—from paycheck to paycheck. She says her feeling is "when you get money, you've got to spend it, because it won't last long."

In many black families of a certain generation, money was rarely, if ever, talked about. Unlike whites, who often sit around and discuss the stock market and other forms of investment at the dinner table, many of us were never exposed to frank discussions about money. As a result, you may have come up without a clear understanding of how to manage your finances, how to use credit wisely, or how to save for the future.

Show Me the Money

No matter the financial legacy you inherited, it's never too late to become money-savvy. The key to getting a handle on it is first to organize your finances. Sure, you know how much you make and you know your monthly outlay for major bills, such as your rent, house note, or car payment. But that's not enough. You need to determine where your money is going every month before you can set up a strategy to reduce your debt or invest more wisely. That means developing a spending plan, also known in some circles as a budget. Budget. The very word may be the barrier between you and financial success. It carries the connotation of self-denial and regret. And it seems to scream, "I can't really afford to live the way I want to, so I have to make a bunch of sacrifices." While a spending plan says, "I can get the stuff I want; I just need to figure out how to do it efficiently."

A spending plan works not only because it encourages discipline and promotes organization, but because it will help you catch the twenty bucks here and the fifty bucks there that manage to slip through your fingers. We all want to get the most out of our money. We all want to live better, save more, enjoy life's pleasures.

Well, a spending plan and all of its elements represent the baby steps that break those big dreams into realistic, doable accomplishments. In order for any plan to work, it has to be more than a blurry sketch in your head. Your plan has to be written down and have quick and easy yardsticks to keep track of your progress.

I'll show you what I mean. Take a clean sheet of paper right now and write down where you spent your money last month. Consult your checkbook, bank statements, whatever you need to. Once you've recorded everything, add up the total and compare it to your net pay for the month. Do the numbers match up evenly? Probably not. If you're like most of us, there are probably large chunks between what you made and what you recall spending. That's money you could perhaps have invested in the stock market or used to treat yourself to that spa weekend you've been wanting to take. Now do you see why you need a spending plan?

Here are eight other solid reasons to create a spending plan:

✦   To rid yourself of debt

✦   To live according to your means

✦   To plan for a major expense, like buying a home, paying for college, or taking a grand vacation

✦   To keep your money from slipping through the cracks

✦   To regain financial stability after a financial setback, like losing a job or getting a divorce

✦   To get your whole family on the same page, financially

✦   To figure out how to accommodate a major lifestyle change, like having a baby or quitting a job

✦   To figure out how to save or invest more money

Spending Plan How-to's

Knowing that a spending plan is a good move may not be enough to move you to action. So before you even begin preparations for your plan, you may want to relax your mind first and pray on it. Take a minute to visualize the positive. Erase from your mind any thoughts of limitation or drudgery. Instead, think about all the good things that are going to manifest in your life because of this proactive stance. Affirm yourself with statements such as "I am blessed with great abundance" and "I can control my financial destiny." Now, let's get busy.

While the numbers may differ, a spending plan's major categories are the same for everyone. You will want to list them as follows:

+ Food

+ Shelter

+ Personal Care

+ Transportation

+ Entertainment

+ Investments/Savings

+ Debt Repayment

+ Business Expenses

+ Miscellaneous

The first step to creating a sound spending plan is simple. You'll need a pocket-size notepad to carry around with you constantly. Every single time you spend money, write it down—whether it's $100 for a pair of shoes, $2 or $3 for a bagel and coffee, or 25 cents for the parking meter. Remember, no expense is too small. Every penny adds up to money spent, money saved, or money wasted. Consider the numbers: If you saved $5 each day for an entire year, you'd end up with $1,825!

It's important that you make no attempt to alter your spending habits as you go through this exercise. What you're trying to do is take a look at exactly where your money goes. Do this every single day for a week. At the end of one week, divide your expenditures into categories, such as "Personal Care"—including manicures, trips to the hairdressers, and such; "Entertainment"—things like video rentals and CD purchases. Multiply the numbers in each category by four. This will give you a rough idea of your monthly spending in these areas.

The next step is to write down the size of your regular monthly bills—rent or mortgage, car note, utilities, day care, and so on. Thumb through your checkbook and bank-card statements for the past few months and try to reconstruct other intermittent outlays, including clothing, birthday presents, and car repairs. Now that you're armed with a snapshot of your monthly spending, you're ready to actually begin creating your spending plan. Take a sheet of paper and write down the major categories as listed previously.

Make sure you're not underestimating your expenses. For example, under "Food," you should list your monthly grocery tab and also the amount you spend eating out for breakfast, lunch, and dinner. "Shelter" should include your monthly housing cost, of course. But you should also add in subcategories like phone cost, gas and electricity, home insurance, household items, and any housekeeping costs. Be realistic when it comes to expenditures for personal care and entertainment; these are areas in which many sisters—in their zeal to cut costs where possible—set the lowest possible allotment. Then they end up feeling either deprived for missing that manicure or guilty for exceeding the plan. Make room for activities like gym membership, clothing, movies, and concerts. Likewise, when it comes to transportation, make an honest tally of what you typically spend on taxis if you rely on them often or car washes or auto maintenance.

Once you've projected how much to spend in each category, subtract your expenses from your net income. If there's money left over, that's fabulous. You can apply it toward savings or put it toward debt repayment. On the other hand, if you come up short, relax. Remind yourself that deficit is a temporary condition that you have the power to change. Examine your spending plan once more. Where can you cut back? Where can you perhaps delay an expense or two?

The Real Deal

Once you've completed your spending-plan projections, the real challenge begins. Hopefully, your little notepad is still handy. As you go through the month, put it to use each day as you record your actual expenditures. This is the same exercise you went through that first week, only this time you'll continue for an entire month. Again, don't sleep on the "small change" you drop here and there for seemingly inconsequential items. Small change fast becomes big money.

At the end of the month you want to make sure your spending plan is working for you. So you need to sit down and look over each category and compare the amount you expected to spend with what you ended up spending.

Here's an outline for making your plan.

Expenses

	PROJECTED	ACTUAL
FOOD		
SHELTER		
PERSONAL CARE		
TRANSPORTATION		
ENTERTAINMENT		
INVESTMENTS/SAVINGS		
DEBT REPAYMENT		
BUSINESS EXPENSES		
MISCELLANEOUS		
TOTAL EXPENSES =		

The moment when you stare at those hard numbers is the moment of truth. There are probably some areas in which you came in over the plan, and there may be categories in which you spent less than you thought you would. Regard the first couple of months of your spending plan as a journey. Remember, one of the main reasons you set out to do this was to get a better idea of where your money is being spent. It is, for example, very common for most people to underestimate the amount of money spent on food. This may be especially true for single sisters. You think to yourself, "Little old me? I barely eat a thing." But if most of your meals are eaten outside the house, be it "cheap" fast food or costlier sit-down meals in restaurants, until now you've probably failed to realize just how much that lil' bit of food is costing you.

As you go forward in the following months, adjust your plan to reflect a more accurate picture of your spending. Now that you're keeping faithful records, you'll be better able to improve your financial health in all aspects. Perhaps, as you see the monthly outlay plainly before you, it's clear that you need to reduce your debt. And you should always be looking for more ways to increase your savings and investment picture.

The first place to start is expenses. Were you surprised at how much you spent compared with your initial projections? If you only barely got through the month with enough cash, you'll need to find ways to cut your expenses. You may also want to reduce your spending in order to save up for a big vacation or other major expense. Don't dismay. You may not need to make wholesale cuts to meet your goal. Look at your plan carefully to determine areas in which you might be able to skim a few bucks here or there. You might be surprised at how quickly those small reductions add up. Need a few pointers? Check out the list below:

Saving Ways

✦ Reduce your long-distance phone bill by e-mailing friends instead of calling.

✦ Eat more meals at home.

✦ Keep an eye out for cheaper forms of entertainment—museums, local parks, the library.

✦ Make a grocery list and stick to it, unless there's a huge sale on something you use often. In that case, stock up on as many of that item as the store will allow.

+ Be a coupon clipper; some grocery stores double their face value, adding up to big food savings.

+ Reduce or eliminate your magazine subscription list. How much time do you really have to read them all?

+ Hide or cut up your credit cards. Each purchase is adding more to your interest payment anyway. So charge absolutely nothing until the balances you have are paid.

+ Review each and every invoice and credit-card statement; watch for hidden fees or erroneous billing.

+ Try switching to some generic or store-brand products when you shop. Some of the products are just as good in quality, and you'll save half the cost of leading brands.

+ Use a pay phone rather than your cell phone whenever possible. In fact, go cellular only in emergencies.

+ Consider making a gift or preparing a homemade meal instead of a pricey store-bought present the next time you celebrate the birthday of a friend or loved one.

+ Examine your service contracts, car and home insurance, long-distance carrier, and others, to see where you might negotiate better rates. Or switch to lower-cost providers.

+ Dip into your savings to reduce your debt; you'll save a mint on interest rates.

+ Be flexible with your travel arrangements. Sometimes taking an off-peak flight can save you as much as $100.

+ Book travel on-line and save a bundle on everything from airfare to hotels and car rentals.

✦ If you're carrying a credit-card balance on clothes purchases, don't allow yourself to buy so much as a scarf until you pay off the last outfit.

Digging Out of Debt

I was at a comedy show once when a brother let loose with a joke that had the whole place howling. There's a big difference, he said, between the way black women and white women shop. When a white woman approaches the cash register, she assembles all her purchases and lays them across the counter. Then, with the utmost confidence, she whips out a gold card and declares, "Charge it." On the other hand, we sisters, he said, walk somewhat meekly toward the sales associate, gingerly place our items down, and rifle through our wallet. As we thumb through credit card after credit card, we finally hand one over. And as the cash register begins to hum, we get to praying, "Oh, Lord. Please, Lord, let it go through."

Sound familiar? Maybe it's not you. But surely you know someone who is a certifiable credit-card junkie, waving around plastic as though it were free money. And unfortunately, that is how charges are often made, frequently and impulsively as though there were no repercussions. Then the bills start to come. And they keep coming and coming until they pile up to form a seemingly insurmountable pile.

Experts will tell you that there's a very simple way to stop the madness: Stop charging.

But for some that's easier said than done. Think back to the start of this chapter and look over your latest credit-card statement. How many of the purchases on it were bought as a result of need and sound planning? More than likely a fair number of the transactions were "emotional buys." You know what I'm talking about. Maybe you had a fight with your man. A project at work fell through. You tell yourself, "It's Friday. I've had a rough week, and a new pair of shoes will cheer me up."

When shopping becomes a crutch, a way of dealing with anger, anxiety, or hurt feelings, you're in danger of creating a debt cycle that may be difficult to break out of. If you're in so deep that you don't know where to begin, don't hesitate to get help. A financial therapist or an organization such as Debtors Anonymous may be for you. You might also check out your local telephone directory for a nonprofit credit-counseling service; they can help you overcome mounting debt woes. For example, most cities have a branch of the Consumer Credit Counseling Service (1-800-388-CCCS). The initial consultation is free.

Once you've gotten to the bottom of why you're in debt, you can start to dig yourself out of it. There's no time like the present. Begin by saying to yourself, "Today I will pay for everything on a cash basis." When you think about making a purchase, make it only if you can cover the price with cash or a check. Almost immediately you will find that you buy more modestly. Studies prove that when people use credit cards, they tend to spend more because the plastic doesn't seem like real money. The simple act of not charging will reap instant benefits. Your total debt load will begin to shrink, because as you pay off your balances, you'll be paying less in interest. But don't stop there. Here are some other ways to tackle your debt:

+ Figure out exactly how much debt you're in (many of us don't even know!) by listing all of your creditors on a piece of paper. Record what you owe on each card and any other important information, including the credit limit on each, your monthly minimum payment, current finance charge, late-payment fees, and interest rates. You'll probably be shocked once you see the numbers. Total all your debt. Finally, for each creditor, divide the balance you owe by your total debt. This will give you an indication of what to pay off first.

✦ Take advantage of some of the low-interest credit-card offers around these days. Transfer higher interest card balances to lower-interest cards. But be careful; make sure the card to which you're transferring doesn't carry an annual fee or any other hidden charges.

✦ Pay more than the minimum balance on each of your cards. If you're carrying a total balance of $3,000 on a card that charges 18 percent interest, paying the minimum required— or $60—means it will take you more than thirty years to get out of debt! If you pay just a little more per month, say $75, you can be out of debt in about five years and save nearly $6,000 in interest!

✦ If illness, loss of wages, or some other financial hardship makes it impossible to pay your creditors, nothing is more important than communication. Each creditor has its own policy. So make no assumptions. And don't wait until you've fallen behind several months; contact every creditor immediately. Arrange a payback plan, but be realistic; don't make any promises you can't keep.

Repairing Your Credit

Even with the most conscientious efforts, once spending has spun out of control, it can be very difficult to keep debtors off your trail. Threatening invoices begin flooding your mailbox, intimidating bill collectors jam your phone at all times of the day and night. And before long your credit rating plummets. Some sisters don't even realize what's up with credit ratings until it is too late. After years of saving they discover once they sit across from a banker or mortgage broker that their poor credit rating could make it impossible to own a home. That's why, whether you've been in financial trouble or not, it's a good idea to know what your credit report looks like. It will list all of your bank cards, charge accounts, and other debts over the past seven years, as well as indicate whether you've made timely payments. Big offenses like liens, foreclosures, and bankruptcies will appear. But so will any type of payment delinquency. There are three major credit bureaus, and all of them will send you a copy of your report free of charge if you request it within 60 days of being turned down for credit. Otherwise, they will charge you about ten dollars. Believe me, it's worth it.

Just call or visit a credit bureau's Web site to find out what is required. You may be asked for information like your Social Security number, birth date, names of current and previous employers, and a list of addresses over the past five years. Once you get your hands on your report, review it carefully. There may be mistakes. If you do find an error, note it on the form, make a copy, and mail it back to the credit bureau. You should also contact the other two; they often share information.

The Three Major Credit Bureaus

Equifax Information Service Center: 1-800-685-1111

Trans Union Corporation: 1-800-916-8800

Experian Consumer Assistance (formerly TRW):
1-800-682-7654

Bad Credit—Now What?

Relax. They did away with debtors' prisons long ago. There's nothing you can do to actually remove your past mistakes from the record. But with a little time and lots of dedication you can become credit-worthy once again. The one exception is bankruptcy. Jane Bryant Quinn, syndicated money columnist and author of *Making the Most of Your Money*, says, "Creditors like to see people fight their way out of debt. They hate bankruptcies."

Once you become aware of your less-than-sterling credit report, commit yourself to repairing the damage as quickly as possible. It sounds obvious, but the first thing you need to do is begin paying all your bills on time. Try the following strategies as well:

+ Pay off any old bills, even if the card issuer has suspended your account. Back bills don't go away just because the notices stop coming.

+ Address the errors on your credit report.

+ If there's something on your credit report that you have since resolved—like a sixty-day delinquency from several years ago—inform the credit bureau. That explanation will become part of your file.

+ Make sure the credit bureau has removed anything that dates back more than seven years. For bankruptcies the time frame is ten years.

+ Take steps to reduce your overall indebtedness so that you're not paying any more than 40 percent of your monthly income to creditors.

Savings Sense

Once you've dealt successfully with your debt, you're ready to launch into a serious savings and investment program. If you've made a thorough review of your spending plan, you should have a clear sense of your savings picture. Are you saving at least 10 percent of your monthly take-home pay on a consistent basis? Or is savings simply an afterthought, the cash you stow away once in a while if you run out of purchase desires for the month?

Remember the sister living in the fast lane with her designer gear and high-profile style? She's a mere paycheck or two away from financial ruin. Don't let that be you. Experts say you should stash the equivalent of three to six months in expenses to ensure a safe cushion in the event of an emergency or sudden loss in wages. This rule applies across the board, regardless of your income/expenses ratio. And it doesn't count hard-to-access monies like the funds in your 401(k) or profit-sharing plans at work. We're talking about cold, liquid cash. Is your reserve at or near the recommended level? If not, don't get discouraged. What's most important is that you make a start and make saving automatic. It may sound silly, but saving even as little as five or ten dollars a month, consistently, is better than nothing.

Make your savings plan real by setting purchasing goals for yourself, like Christmas presents, a vacation, or a car. Then set aside a certain amount of money from each savings deposit for that particular purchase.

For some sisters, saving money is like a herculean task. Again, I suggest you try to figure out what's behind those barriers that stand in your way. If you're single, could it be that you think a man will eventually come to your emotional and financial rescue, eliminating the need for you to look out for your own future? Perhaps you're married and you're ducking the responsibility because you regard it as your man's role. Or you believe the joint savings account you two share is enough. It's not. I'm not suggesting that you sabotage the financial goals you and your husband have set, but it is crucial that every sister have a little nest egg of her own.

If you simply lack the discipline to incorporate saving into your regular routine, investigate a payroll-savings plan that may be offered by your employer. Or try some of the programs below. They are five easy ways to keep your savings regular (with as little as twenty-five dollars a month).

+ **EMPLOYEE BENEFIT SAVINGS.** Also known as 401(k)s. These let you invest a percentage of your pretax salary in stock, fixed-income, or money-market funds.

+ **U.S. SAVINGS BONDS DEDUCTION.** Nearly fifty thousand companies participate; the withheld amount is invested in a Series EE savings bond ($15,000 annual maximum).

+ **MUTUAL FUND AUTOMATIC.** Based on your instructions, a fund company will transfer a set amount of money from your checking account to one of its funds every month.

+ **MUTUAL FUND REINVESTMENT.** Automatically reinvest the dividends and capital gains paid out by your mutual fund and watch your profits grow.

+ **STOCK DIVIDEND REINVESTMENT PLAN.** Offered by many publicly traded companies, this plan allows you to take your stock dividends and use them to buy more stock.

Taking Stock

Many sisters mistakenly believe that because they don't make much money, they should avoid the stock market and other investments. The truth is, it's a good idea to start an investment strategy early on to make the most of your money, then build on it as your finances expand. The bull market, as it is known when stocks are particularly hot, has created a population of investment millionaires, or folks whose net worth has increased dramatically purely by letting their money "sit" in the market. Like most of you, I did not grow up with any knowledge of the stock market. My dad barely trusted the local savings and loan, much less the cryptic gyrations of international financial markets.

Rest assured, the stock market is nothing to fear. Through bull and bear (lean) times, the market has outpaced the rate of inflation by about 8 percent each year since 1926. That's a better return than you can yield from any other legal financial investment. If invested wisely, stocks can deliver returns that dwarf the paltry 3 percent gains of most savings accounts and certificates of deposit. There is, of course, some risk involved. But stocks can be very beneficial as financial tools if you're willing to stay committed for the long haul.

If you're a market watcher and knowledgeable about certain industries, you may want to approach stock purchases on an individual basis, buying those you think will turn in the best performance. What many people choose to do is trade stocks through a broker or investment club. By far the most popular way of getting into the market these days is through mutual funds. And unless you're extremely savvy at reading and analyzing balance sheets and research reports or can afford to pay commissions to a leading professional, they're the best way to go.

You've probably heard of funds like Fidelity, Dreyfus, and Oppenheimer. These are simply pools of money that individual investors contribute toward. A fund manager takes the pool and invests it. The advantage of funds is that they offer professional money management. They take your investments—which can start at as little as fifty dollars—and diversify them, while at the same time balancing your risks.

Whether you go it alone or choose a fund, there are a few basic investment principles you should keep in mind:

✦ HANG IN THERE. Don't be swayed by the market's ups and downs. You should invest with at least a ten-year outlook in mind.

✦ TIMING ISN'T ALWAYS EVERYTHING. The old cliché, "buy low, sell high" makes a great sound bite, but few of us have the savvy to hit the market so precisely. And even the so-called experts are often wrong. Stocks rise more often than they fall, so the lesson here is "stay in it to win it."

✦ MAKE INVESTING A HABIT. Some portion of each paycheck should go toward your mutual fund. There's no such thing as a "bad market" for investing, because stocks will continue to rise and fall.

✦ DON'T PANIC. There will be times when you make a lot of money from your investments, and there will be times when the payoff is lean or nonexistent. Time is your friend. Stay the course; don't make any rash moves.

✦ PATIENCE IS THE NAME OF THE GAME. A wise man once said, "You can get poor quickly. However, getting rich takes time."

Mind Over Money

As you put the many financial principles outlined in this chapter into practice, be clear about one thing: You can be a financial success. Glinda Bridgforth, sister financial counselor and author of *Girl, Get Your Money Straight,* recommends that we remind ourselves of this fact with prayer and affirmation. She says the affirmative actions below—which you can post on the fridge, your mirror, computer, or anywhere as a gentle reminder—will help you take the steps necessary to create greater wealth. I'm a believer.

+ I know there is abundance in the universe, and I will live comfortably.

+ I will learn from my past financial mistakes and move forward to make better choices.

+ I am committed to making a monthly spending plan to improve my financial health.

+ I will track and analyze my spending, examining the motives behind each purchase.

+ I will make time to honor and take care of myself every day and be grateful for what I have.

+ I will resist the urge to splurge.

Chapter 6

A SEXY SOUL MATE

He moves you, grooves you, "gets" you. So where the hell is he? Whether we're searching for our love thang in the darkness of a smoke-filled club or staring our man dead in the face each morning but not really seeing him, all of us have asked ourselves the same questions at one time or another: "Is this it?" "Does it have to be so hard?" And "Is it me, or is this brother simply impossible to find/reach?"

In a nutshell the answers are as follows: "No." "No." And "No."

Soulful relationships don't just happen. Given the generations black folks have spent struggling to overcome the deeply wounding effects of hardship and oppression, relationships between brothers and sisters require work. Forced to carry the weight of history—with all its fears and insecurities—our brothers face a daily onslaught of bigotry, as do we. It's not always easy leaving the world's subtle and not-so-subtle slights at the door each evening or in your work bag while you do happy hour. What men and women both want and need most of all is to feel the welcoming warmth of a loving pair of arms to shelter us from society's harsh realities. Yet that's not always what we get, and it sure as hell is not often what we give.

Whether we're trying to find that special someone to share our life with or whether we're in a relationship or marriage, many of us find ourselves simply wondering, "What does a sister have to do to get some love around here?" The short answer: We have to learn just *how* to give love and get it in return. It's something of an art, so let's start from the beginning.

Love and the Single Sister

I heard Star Jones, the bold and beautiful cohost of daytime television's *The View*, reveal a few of her New Year's resolutions last year. I was particularly struck by one. Concerning her well-known desire to get married and start a family, she had this to say: "I've decided to stop looking for Mr. Right and let Mr. Right find me." What a powerful affirmation of self-worthiness! Here sister-friend was on national TV telling the world, "Hey, I'm all that. So let a brother step to me and discover how lucky he is."

I knew a girl with that same kind of attitude when I was back in college. She never seemed pressed to "find" a man, yet she was always surrounded by several sexy suitors. The irony is that she was no beauty queen by most people's standards, and though she was smart and sweet, if you got on her wrong side, she'd cuss you out in a New York minute. You're probably thinking she was a closet freak, right? Not so. I knew her roommate very well, and she swears that she never stayed out all night, and if a guy stayed over their place, he and this sister would fall asleep on the couch after talking half the night. When the rest of us looking to get hooked up would press this brother-magnet to reveal her secret, she would simply shrug and say, "There *is* no secret. Just don't stress it." It took me a couple of years, but then I discovered there was truth in her words.

Men do enjoy the freedom of being with someone who doesn't stress them or the relationship, someone who smiles and laughs easily. What's more, there is something to the way this sister walked out into the world expecting men to be attracted to her. She was very comfortable in her own skin, and that's the vibe she sent out. By contrast, I can remember trying to interest a male friend in a girlfriend of mine who was, at least physically and on paper, everything one might think a man would want. Yet after a few dates, brotherman seemed disinterested. I asked him what was up. His reply: "Your girl's got a big D for 'desperate' stamped across her forehead."

Too many single women have themselves locked in this supplicant role in which they are almost begging to be loved. This needy mentality manifests itself in countless ways—jockeying with other sisters for a man's attention, hooking up with brothers who are undeserving of our affections, and staying in relationships that do not honor us.

Alone Doesn't Have to Mean Lonely

Recognize that if you're single, that does not mean you need to feel loveless or unfulfilled. We don't need to go searching for love. Love—true love—begins inside. This may sound trite, and you may be mumbling under your breath, "Of course I love myself." But think about it. How often do you engage in the kind of self-defeating patterns of language that serve to diminish your uniqueness? For some it happens as soon as they look in the mirror each morning: "My hair is too nappy" or "My legs are too skinny" or "My butt is too big." How are you going to find someone to love you and accept you for you when you can't even do it yourself? Rather than drown yourself in negativity, give *yourself* some love as you start each day. Look in the mirror and say, "*Yes!* I've got it going on." If you feel awkward saying it aloud, at the very least think it, and for sure believe it. Our thoughts and words are potent predictors of what can and will manifest in our lives. Quite simply, we are what we think we are. As you work on loving yourself from the inside out, reprogram your mind-set. Get your heart and mind prepared for the loving man you will soon attract. When you send out positive energy, not only will you feel much better about yourself, you'll find that men respond to you in a whole new way.

Are You Love-able?

Whether you're hoping for a love connection or you're already hooked up, check yourself to make sure you're truly able to love. If you have trust issues or other intimacy barriers lurking in your emotional psyche, any union—no matter how righteous the brother—could be doomed from the start.

Do some honest reflecting. Ask yourself if your spirit and heart are open to the idea of someone coming into your life. Or are you angry—either at yourself or at the last man you dealt with? When you are love-able or relationship-ready, three things are true of you:

1. You love the person you are and the place you're in right now.

2. You're open, comfortable with change, and accepting of change and growth in others.

3. You respect all the lessons you've learned, even the most painful ones.

As a people, many African-Americans lack a practical frame of reference when it comes to relationships with the opposite sex, because we might not have grown up with examples of healthy unions. Of course, this can be a problem for nonblacks, too, but the situation is far more acute for brothers and sisters. In the same way that we as blacks are vulnerable to greater health risks, our relationships face increased pressures. To begin with, during slavery our love relationships were not honored or respected. Our families were wantonly ripped asunder. Even in our parents' or grandparents' generations, conditions were only marginally improved. Many of them grew up in the shadow of Jim Crow segregation. Our men were the last hired and first fired. Even when employed, whether as professionals or laborers, they lived in a time of great economic instability for African-Americans. And financial insecurity can be even more debilitating than joblessness to a man's self-esteem. It's no wonder why, according to the United States Census, in the late 1960s and early seventies, only about 65 percent of black households consisted of two parents.

Historically, what many of us sisters have sadly lacked in our formative years is the boundless and unconditional love of a male figure. With Daddy distant, absent altogether, or, even worse, making intermittent appearances, black girls go into the world as women with no concept or appreciation of what a man's strength and affection feel like. So we grope around in search of some semblance of what we think is male love, sometimes settling for sex without the respect or power without the tenderness.

If yours was one of the families that managed to stay together, don't think you've come away unscathed. Even in marriages that remain intact, children can grow up with unhealthy images of couplehood. This is especially the case when there is verbal and/or physical abuse, emotional abandonment, constant bickering, or even less obvious conditions like a paucity of affection. We carry with us the relationship "models" we grew up with—good and bad. And these models inform our own dealings with the opposite sex. That's why it's important to come to terms with them. I admit it, this is not pleasant stuff to deal with. It's hard to delve into the past, especially when it means we may be critical of our parents in the process. But that is not what this self-reflection is about. We all know that in most cases our folks did the best they knew how. Looking back at the messages you received from them is in no way meant to lay blame upon them or disrespect them. It's simply meant to instruct us as we go forward into relationships of our own. Maybe now is not the time for you to do this kind of soul-searching. But just to give you an idea of how important it is to do so, ask yourself the questions below. Take a minute to really ponder your answers, perhaps write them down in your journal. You may be surprised by what you discover.

+ How do you define love?

+ Is love fair? Does love hurt?

+ Do you believe you'll ever find a soul mate?

+ What did you learn about love from your parents?

+ How has that influenced your relationships with men?

+ How would you describe your overall feelings about black men?

+ Have you been able to maintain a long-term relationship? Why?

✦ Do you find yourself in relationship after relationship with the same type of man?

Your answers—or lack thereof—should give you some idea of just how love-able you are. If, for example, you choose the same man over and over, you are not relationship-ready. You may tell yourself that attracting the same guy is something that is happening *to* you. But it's really the result of what is happening *in* you. Letting the same man into your life repeatedly is a pretty sure indication that you remain the same woman. That is, you have not shown a willingness or ability to grow or learn from your mistakes. Folks—whether male or female—come into our lives in order to teach us something about ourselves. Through each encounter we should be learning just what we are made of. How able are we to empathize with others? How open are we to sharing, to loving? Often we don't have a clue, and without thoughtful introspection and self-help, we don't have a chance.

Love Busters

We sisters are complex beings. Admittedly, we have issues, especially when it comes to matters of the heart. Some of us have had our hearts shattered into a million tiny pieces. Many of us haven't, yet carry on relationships based on the assumption that we will. It's not that we're gluttons for punishment. It's not that we don't want—and deserve—good loving. The problem is that we are, as a group, conditioned self-saboteurs. Whether it's our anger, our general distrust of the male species, or—the biggest culprit—our Strong Black Woman armor, we have the uncanny ability to chase love away with rebellious acts of sabotage.

If you're operating under the assumption that all black men are no good, for example, that they only want one thing or that you must dog or be dogged, then you're probably what psychologist and relationship expert Dr. Gwendolyn Goldsby Grant calls a "dead-spirit sister." "Dead spirits attract deadbeats," says the popular author of *Essence*'s "Between Us" column. I love talking to my sister. She delivers it to you straight, no chaser.

The dead-spirit sister comes by her affliction honestly, explains the good doctor. She inherits it from her mama, who got it from *her* mama, and so on. These black male stereotypes were handed down from generation to generation and make up the tragedy of our history. Beginning three hundred years ago we subconsciously began to accept and incorporate into our psyches the white man's myths and criminations about the "cunning," "dangerous," and "sex-crazed" black man. Such lies destroyed our love affairs then, and, experts say, to this day they continue to cast a pall over relations between sisters and brothers. That's why when you were growing up, you may have received messages such as "Keep your dress down; boys just want to get in your pants" rather than "Lovemaking can be beautiful; trust your heart." Whether they were uttered by your mother, your aunts, or their girlfriends, if you're like most sisters, you surely were fed an earful of statements like "That Negro is no damn good" and "You can't trust him as far as you can throw him."

For the most part, the story of our male-female relationships has been set against a backdrop of hard luck and heartbreak—not happily-ever-after bliss. So it should come as little surprise when our love affairs fail. In love, just as in life, we reap what we speak—making our own reality. And failure is preprogrammed or prophesied into our love lives. As a result, says Dr. Grant, we sisters perpetrate a series of sabotage maneuvers to keep ourselves from the love we want. "Once you've already prophesied something, it's going to come to pass, even if you have to manipulate the situation to make the prophecy come true," she says. To that end, each of us has her own particular method of sabotage. Most of us have a single favorite, though some have a smorgasbord of self-defeating acts. According to Grant, they include the following:

✦ **MISS EVIL JEAN.** We all know one, if not several. Such a sister is known for telling a Negro where to go and how to get there at the slightest provocation. To her mind, all men are prone to lies and trickery, so she adopts her "Don't mess with me" stance from day one, to keep brotherman in line. Her coldness, however, is really just a shield. She's using conflict to deny her inner pain, trying to "protect" herself from getting hurt. Of course, in the process, she gets no love at all.

✦ **SMOTHER LOVE.** This sister has no life and is so needy, she has to be with her man 24/7 in order to feel secure. As the old folks say, "She can't breathe unless she's up in that man's mouth." She masks her insecurity in a blanket of "love," trying to convince her mate that it's her powerful affection for him that makes her want him near so often. There are certain brothers who might find this unhealthy attachment flattering for a while—but only a short while. Eventually this sister's smothering tactics will suffocate her man and drive him away.

✦ **FAMILY FEUD.** Maybe it's his mother, maybe it's his brother, his sister, or his kids. But this sister-saboteur views her man's close primary relationships as a threat. As a result, she attempts to "win" him from his family. She finds fault with people closest to him and blames them for the shortcomings in their love trust. The reality is, no amount of competing will ever triumph over family ties. No matter what happens between a man and woman, his mother will still be his mother, his kids will still be his kids.

✦ **PUSSY PLAY.** Albeit crude, this sabotage method works several ways. But in the final analysis, it always comes down to using sex as a tool. And it almost always leads to a breakdown in intimacy. In an extremely common display of this behavior, a sister is ready to give "it" up before the relationship has even had a chance to bloom. And she thinks freakish romps will ensure his devotion. On the flip side, there's the sister who withholds sex, dishing it out only when it can "win" her something—usually something monetary—in return.

- ✦ **MISS I-DON'T-NEED-NOBODY.** This is most often the sabotage of choice for the Strong Black Woman. This sister is so independent, so no-nonsense, that she simply can't suffer a man who tries to do for her. She may or may not articulate it, but she makes it clear in no uncertain terms that a brother is dispensable. It's damn near impossible for such a sister to demonstrate any hint of vulnerability. With almost every act of affection or chivalry, she seems to say, "Get out the way. I'll do it myself."

The saddest thing about saboteurs is that they're rarely aware of their methods of madness. Despite the love busters they perpetrate, these sisters continue to wonder why they can't find or keep a good man, why true love seems to elude them. More often than not they actually fear the intimacy they crave. So they create barriers to keep themselves from having to expose their inner selves.

What's more, usually these sabotaging sisters are in intense emotional pain; scars from decades-old wounds remain unhealed. If you approach one of them about her self-defeating ways, you may get a response like "Yeah, my father booked when I was five" or "Daddy was a womanizer." Followed by "But that was a long time ago. It doesn't affect me today." In truth, for better or worse, every major event in our lives plays a role in shaping our personalities, informing our fears and anxieties, and either building or damaging our self-images. The challenge for each of us is to recognize and rectify the issues in our lives that keep us from giving and receiving love.

Review the following lessons to make yourself love-ready:

- **LOVE HAS NO FEAR.** Recognize that no one can bring love into your life and, conversely, no one can take it away. A man may choose to walk, but that doesn't mean love has gone out the door with him. When a sister tells me she's in love but she's scared, I know that what she really means is that she's afraid the object of her affection won't love her back. Even if that should be the case, the love inside you is still valid and important.

- **SOMETIMES YOU NEED TO FLIP THE SCRIPT.** In the movies, boy meets girl. They fall madly in love and a hot, on-screen round of passion unfolds before our eyes. But as sisters, we need to work past the celluloid fantasy. Good sex, romantic lines, and fancy gifts do not a true love make. If you see your own relationships playing out like scripted performances, where you fall for some of the same things over and over, it's time to take stock and get a grip. Learn to value and appreciate the intangible elements of friendship and compatibility.

- **FOREVER IS A LONG TIME.** Relationships last for as long as two people need them to. Accept the fact that not all relationships are meant to endure. At a vulnerable point in your life, you may become involved with someone who is a caregiver. As time passes, you may grow stronger and find that his need to nurture no longer fulfills you. There's nothing wrong with that. There's a natural ebb and flow to all relationships. What's most important is that, as a sister who is relationship-ready, you're cognizant of your needs at any given time and you know when they are or are not being met.

✦ **RELATIONSHIP INVENTORY IS A MUST.** Take time out to reflect on your relationships. If you keep a journal, each day for a month write down something you've learned from a relationship—be it with a friend, a co-worker, or a love interest. You might write about something the two of you discussed or just a certain vibe you picked up during an encounter. When you reminisce or look back on your notes, assess how much you grew, how much you gave of yourself, how much you received. An exercise like this can do several things. It can help you sift out unhealthy patterns in your own behavior, and it can also help you determine which of your relationships are good for you and which are toxic.

Becoming love-ready is not limited to romantic or sexual encounters. Each and every relationship you experience has power, the power to heal you or hurt you, empower you or embitter you. Read Chapter 8, "Loving Family and Friends," to find out how your relationships with parents, siblings, other family members, and friends help shape the person you are and form the foundation upon which most love relationships will be supported.

Relationship readiness is not something that can be hurried or compressed. It won't happen overnight. But it is surely worth the journey. When you're emotionally and spiritually primed to receive intimacy, you're far more attuned to your relationship needs. The more informed you are, the better the decisions you will make. In short, the truly love-ready have greater success in relationships; they find it far easier to drop relationship zeroes and hook up with their heroes!

Kissing Frogs and Other Myths for Single Sisters

By the time most of us reach adulthood, we think we have a pretty good idea of our ideal mate. We've probably "seen" him in our dreams, where we've danced at our wedding, then settled into the white-picket-fenced house—all before the first date. I'm going to venture to guess that this fantasy loverman has the strong, classic good looks of Denzel Washington, the ageless charm and savoir faire of Harry Belafonte, and the chiseled body of supermodel Tyson. And to top it all off, brotherman is *paid*; he's got bank like Michael Jordan. Now, maybe I've missed a few small details, but for the most part I bet I'm pretty on target when it comes to the man most sisters are dreaming of. I would never encourage you to settle for less than what you desire in any area of your life, but may I suggest that you open yourself up to a somewhat different résumé? Let's remember that looks fade and muscles grow soft. And here's one other important fact: in the mid-nineties, *The Wall Street Journal* reported that during the economic boom of the eighties the rate of black female professionals soared. By 1992 our numbers had topped an estimated two hundred thousand. During that same period, however, the numbers of black men in professional careers actually decreased. What this obviously means is that there are fewer high-income brothers among whom to choose. What's more, a brother's occupation or bank account is no indication of his character. An honest, compassionate, hardworking carpenter trumps an arrogant, philandering stock analyst in my book any day.

The sister who overlooks the UPS deliveryman or the transit worker could be passing up happiness, because her blind fantasies and preconceptions won't allow her to see past a uniform that doesn't include a tie. These sisters may say they're looking for a good man with whom to share a loving relationship, but what's more important to them is a trophy or showpiece mate who will impress their friends and boost their status. Worse still is when a sister gets involved with a brother beneath her materialistic standards, with hopes of changing him. She sees his laboring skill as raw material she will use to mold him into her ideal man. She presses him to attend or finish college, even when he displays little interest in doing so. She clips articles and buys books, offering unsolicited career advice. And at nearly every opportunity she prods and prompts her man to improve himself, unwittingly sending out the message that who he is isn't good enough.

You may not be a fixer-upper specialist in the area of career enhancement, but if you enter a relationship with a man because "he's got potential," you're probably just as guilty. You're not likely to change a man to suit you. When the best thing you can say about the brother is that he has "potential," what you're really saying is that you're not happy with who he is right now. If that's the case, no amount of self-help, pep-talking will change matters. Consider the long and complex journey that shaped us into what and who we are today. You received messages and influences from your parents that informed your personality, your goals, and your values. Do you think decades-long impressions can be erased by the lofty ambitions of a "well-meaning" partner?

Where Can He Be?

Once you've done the inner work to be ready to give and receive love, then comes the footwork. I remember my years of livin' single, and a lot of my friends are flying solo right now. So I know the words to the sister-girl sad song: "Where are all the good brothers?" Well, don't trip on the statistics. Yes, too many of our men are caught up in the web of the criminal justice system. And yes, they are often victims of violent crime. But you don't need to concern yourself with the hundreds who are, for whatever reason, unattainable. You're not the U.S. Marines; you only need *one* good man.

But he's unlikely to come knocking on your door, saying, "Hi. I heard you were taking applications." A lot of you may bristle at the thought of "looking" for a man. But think of it like my girl Star Jones—you're not looking; you're just making it easier for him to find you. So get up off your happy hips and get moving. Stop thinking that you have to have a man to go to the movies, to go to dinner, or to go anywhere for that matter. If you can't enjoy your own company, who else will? And in the process, Mr. Right just may find you.

Your best chances of connecting with someone with whom you share common interests is to go to the places that most interest *you*. Got a thing for poetry? Enroll in a poetry-writing workshop and check out some of the spoken-word clubs around town. Are you a sports junkie? Join a fitness center and get involved in large competitions, such as an athletic corporate challenge. In addition to the kinds of activities in which you excel, keep yourself open to new experiences as well. Has watching Tiger Woods light up the fairway piqued an interest in golf? Take a few lessons. Likewise, you may not be a budding Serena or Venus Williams, but if they've inspired you with their strength and form, why not try your hand at tennis lessons? The point is, searching for a soul mate can—and should—be about more than the hunt. That kind of single-minded focus will only leave you empty. By becoming active and opening up to exciting new adventures, you're adding new and interesting dimensions to your life. And when you're doing something you enjoy doing, you can't help but send out a positive and energetic vibe, making you more attractive and interesting to everyone around you. For more ways to have some fun and at the same time increase your chances of making a love connection, check out the following list of suggestions I've compiled from sophisticated seekers:

Fifty Places to Meet Your Match

Book signings

Basketball games

Church/choir

Professional organizations

Coed book clubs

Dance classes

Continuing-education courses

Libraries

Block or neighborhood association

Beach

Art galleries

Political rallies

Volunteer organizations

Coffeehouses

Weddings

Shopping malls

Black History Month events

Billiard halls

A jogging path you take frequently

A card party, where you and each girlfriend bring a platonic male friend

Sports bars

Gym

Flea markets

On-line dating services

Alumni events

Spoken-word events

Professional conventions

Roller skating

Gas stations

Hardware stores

Housewarming parties

Car shows

Amusement parks

Black expos

Kwanzaa parties

Laundromat (most
attached men don't do
their own laundry)

Supermarkets (observe the
cart for signs of single
life—small portions,
frozen dinners)

Yard sales

Do-it-yourself stores, like
Home Depot

Subway platforms or bus
stops

Waiting areas at airports

Ski parties

Golf outings

Dog runs in the park

Adventure vacations

Happy hour

Tattoo parlors
(if you dare)

Record stores

Electronics stores (ask for
help selecting a stereo or
TV)

Menswear stores like
Brooks Brothers that
offer women's clothes, too

Foolproof Flirting

You're out there, and you think you've spotted him. He's sitting across the room. You've been in the same art-appreciation class for weeks, and brotherman always has something insightful to add to the group discussions. Now what?

Here are six surefire ways to get his attention and let him know you're interested:

✦ **SMILE A WHILE.** A single brother I've known since college recently told me about what he and the boys call "the evil sister" syndrome: you say "hello" and she rolls her eyes or sighs like she's doing you a favor, he said. It may sound corny, but flashing all thirty-twos is tops when it comes to getting a man's attention.

✦ **LOOK YOUR BEST.** This doesn't mean you need to look as if you just stepped off a runway, but even on the weekends remember that you never know whom you might meet. You should be neat and well groomed at all times.

✦ **COLOR ME BEAUTIFUL.** We all know that when it comes to clothing, black is a classic and chic color. But it's not the friendliest shade in the spectrum. Studies show that men respond to more inviting colors. Among their favorites: aqua, mauve, and red.

✦ **WALK TALL, STAND PROUD.** You don't want to seem high cidity, but a regal walk lets a man see you for the African queen you are. And it says volumes about your power and self-confidence.

✦ **LOSE THE CREW.** Men find it a lot easier to approach a woman who's alone or in the company of just one or two friends. In other words, a pack of your twenty closest girls is not exactly considered neutral territory.

✦ **THE EYES HAVE IT.** When a man you're interested in speaks or looks at you, speak back—with your eyes. Look him in the eye as often as possible for as long as possible. Studies show that peering into his eyes can awaken his primal instincts—triggering the release of a natural endorphin that simulates the feeling of being in love.

Dating Games: Playing to Win

It's on! He's got your digits. You've got his. The next several encounters will either make or break your decision to go forward. Unlike some folks, I don't believe there are any dating "rules"—for sisters or anyone else. But I do believe that there are certain basic tenets of courtesy, warmth, and common sense that some of us have for too long forgotten or ignored.

Because of a lot of the baggage we ourselves bring into our dealings with men—including issues of mistrust and resentment—we often neglect to start each date with a clean slate. At least until he proves to deserve otherwise, treat a man with respect. Be cordial. Be interesting as well as interested. And above all, be yourself. Most of us would probably never roll our eyes toward the sky when meeting a prospective sister-friend for the first time. We would give her the benefit of the doubt. So why cop an attitude as soon as a brother makes his approach? Unless he's being downright disrespectful, there's no need to throw shade. Contrary to some reigning views, being rude or playing hard to get is not a turn-on for most men. If you're Tyra Banks, they may play along for a while, but even then only for a little while. Nick Chiles, co-author with his wife, Denene Millner, of *What Brothers Think, What Sistahs Know*, explains, "We want you to be friendly to us. We want you to talk to us. We want you to act like you want us to talk to you. We don't want you to play hard to get, because it's a bore and it confuses the hell out of us."

With that in mind, here are six guidelines to successful dating:

- ✦ **DON'T STALK A BROTHER.** There's a fine line between letting him know you're interested and chasing him down. Don't do all the calling, paging, and planning. If you do, you'll never know his true intentions. Is he interested or just taking what's put out so conveniently before him?

✦ **CHECK YOUR SAMSONITE.** On your first few dates he does not need to know about emotional baggage like your therapy sessions or the details of your failed marriage. Save the deep stuff for the later stages of your relationship as it unfolds. Otherwise you'll scare him and send him off screaming "TMI"—Too Much Information. He'll be headed for the hills.

✦ **DON'T FRONT.** In the end, putting on airs or pretending to be something you're not will only get you in trouble. A reasonably intelligent brother can smell a phony a mile away; it's a major turn-off. Besides, you'll find it difficult to keep up the false pretenses over the long term.

✦ **KEEP DOING YOUR THING.** Many sisters fall into a trap of meeting a man and putting everything else (including their girlfriends and other interests) on pause. When the romance fizzles, they're left trying to pick up the pieces of all their other relationships. For your own sake, don't sit idly by the telephone waiting for his call. Ultimately, always being available will make you less desirable, not more.

✦ **LESS BOOT KNOCKING, MORE SOUL ROCKING.** You may want to get your swerve on, but rushing into sex always leads to trouble. Let's face it, first and foremost, sex—especially the real good kind—blurs your senses. After a few rounds it's difficult to tell whether you're falling for his conversation or his other communication skills. In order to stand the test of time, you need to be able to make love to his mind as well as his joystick.

✦ **KNOW WHEN TO SAY WHEN.** Be strong enough to get past the smooth rap and flirtation long enough to really hear what the brother is saying. Is he emotionally healthy? Mentally mature? How does he regard his mother? His sister? His children, if he has any? If he has flaws you know you can't live with, don't hesitate to move on—the sooner the better.

Make It Last

Okay, okay. So you've beaten down your demons and finally opened the door to your heart. It looks like this one's a keeper, or maybe you've even said "I do." In the early stages of your romance, the passion is almost too much for even you to bear. When you two walk down the street, the rest of the world is merely a backdrop to your loving, intimate conversations, enjoyed between kisses. The lovemaking is the hot, no-holds-barred, take-no-prisoners kind you'd previously only read about in steamy novels. Then, suddenly and without warning, it seems the honeymoon draws to a close. One day you can't stop gazing into one another's eyes; the next day you're sitting in silence across from each other at a restaurant wearily forking your entrées around the plate. What happened? Did the love fade? Hardly. You can barely imagine a world without him in it. But a teeny thing called real life has insinuated itself into your starry-eyed love affair. Maybe he's feeling stressed these days because a big company just bought the firm he works for and his future there is uncertain. For your part, life is increasingly complex. Perhaps you're doing the work of two people since your department downsized, and you're worried about your ailing grandmother down south. Times like these are supposed to draw a couple closer together, aren't they? Welcome to Relationships 101. It's that tough lesson we must face when girl meets boy and romance meets reality. It may seem like a kick-ass course at first. But trust me: You can do this.

First you need to recognize that happy couplings don't just

stay that way on their own. Sure, a pair has to have the general elements, like love and compatibility. But there's a lot more to it than that. Success at any endeavor takes work. I don't mean work in the sense of drudgery and toil. I'm talking about the kind of inner work we must all undertake in order to live with another person. There are four basic prerequisites to a sound relationship: communication, acceptance, patience, and humor.

✦ **COMMUNICATION.** It's something you may tire of hearing, but it's true. The first step toward a successful relationship is open and honest communication. Understand that any information you receive from your partner is an opportunity to know him better. In other words, communication is a gift. Resist the urge to interrupt him or defend yourself—even in the midst of an argument—and concentrate on truly hearing your man and trying to understand where his feelings are coming from. Of course, if your man is like most brothers, this requires special skill. Our men are not known as fonts of emotional expression. We'll delve into that later. Meanwhile, work on deepening your appreciation of communicating.

✦ **ACCEPTANCE.** Your sweetie has a heart of gold, but some of his ways drive you to distraction. He puts the milk carton back in the fridge even though there's barely enough left to wet two Cheerios. His idea of a date is a televised Knicks game and two pizzas (one for you). You can do either of two things: You can nag him to death and wait—in vain—for him to come around to your way of thinking. Or you can learn to accept the fact that differences can actually enhance a relationship. Who would've thought chicken and waffles would couple so deliciously?

✦ **PATIENCE.** Both you and your beloved entered your relationship with a set of values and proclivities, some of which may run counter to the notion of living together in harmony. Be patient with yourself as well as with your partner while you two get yourselves accustomed to relating to each other. There may be times when, despite your great love, you two don't like each other very much. If you value the relationship and want it to last, don't jet at the slightest sign of trouble.

✦ **HUMOR.** There is a bit of humor in just about every situation. Look for it; in fact, relish it. Laughter is great for whatever ails you. I know I said relationships are work. But don't get too, too serious. Remember, all work and no play is dull, dull, dull. Sometimes you can use your sense of humor to defuse a situation or help your man recover from a setback.

Brother-speak: How to Talk So He'll Listen and Listen So He'll Talk

Does this sound familiar? Claiming that he's helping out, your man throws a load of laundry in the wash. Stranger that he is to such routine household chores, he neglects to separate his red Chicago Bulls' T-shirt from the whites, and you come home to find some of your favorite bras and panties dyed Pepto-Bismol pink.

In horror, you yell out, "What the hell happened? You totally ruined my lingerie!"

In frustration and anger, he responds, "You're tripping. It's just underwear. Damn, woman, there's no pleasing you. I can't do nothing right!"

To be sure, in an ideal world, you would have taken time to filter your emotions and then chosen your words more carefully. You might have treated your delicates to a bleach soaking and said something like "Baby, I'm glad to see you pitching in. We have to work on separating colors, though."

If you happen to be one of those sisters blessed with a silver tongue, the kind who can lace even the harshest subjects with honey, God bless your mama for schooling you proper on the ways of men. If you're like the rest of us, the type of sister who—despite her heartfelt love and affection for a brother—seems to get caught up in the heat of the moment and serves up her feelings raw and uncut, then join the club.

Through trial and more error than I care to own up to, I've learned that our words can either build our brothers up or tear them down, just as society has done and continues to do on the regular. The choice is ours to make. We can choose words that spew venom of distrust and humiliation or we can come from a place of love and appreciation.

Have you ever had the pleasure of witnessing the interaction between a matriarch from the old school and her man? If so, I'm sure you heard a lot of "yes, babies" and "sweeties" trip off her tongue. She probably patted his arm or leg often. And looked admiringly as he spoke to others. You may have come away thinking, "Puh-lease, that doting-wifey act is *so* not me. I'm independent."

Now, I'm not suggesting for one minute that we shuck our independence. But what I am saying is that the older generations of women had a secret that a lot of us younger sisters have failed to pick up on: Men eat that kind of stuff up. You should by no means be phony, but do take note. These women knew how to get their men to respond to them, and it didn't involve a whole lot of screaming and put-downs.

Let's face it, sometimes your man honestly deserves to be blessed out. But in most good relationships those times are few. There are many more occasions when his intentions are good; in his own small way he is actually trying to please you. And still, we focus on what our man didn't do. We don't necessarily even have to raise our voices. That one, small criticism, that hint of disapproval, is all he needs to come away feeling deflated and unloved.

This is true for any man (and they call *us* the weaker sex). But it's especially true for our black men. When we deal with our brothers, we must put into context the painful legacy that has been handed down to them from generations of degradation and oppression. This is not to make excuses for them; it's simply to better understand them. Now, I can hear you mumbling under your breath, "I've inherited a painful legacy, too." And I'm feeling you on that point. But the fact of the matter is that we seek our affirmation differently, and often we have an entire network of support from which we draw.

Knowing how to talk to a black man is two parts art (remember the older matriarchs) and one part science—a careful blend of timing, honesty, and tenderness—that makes him feel valid in a world that often does not. Remember, a brother is likely to shed the tough exterior he presents to the world on a very limited basis. As his woman, you're one of the few people he's open to. When you speak to him in a way that validates him, you accomplish many things. For starters, you boost his self-esteem. You also build his trust and comfort level in the relationship. Finally, you encourage him to look for even more ways to please you. And isn't that what we all want?

I've talked to some experts on this topic (Lord knows, I don't have all the answers), and I hope their insights will help you appreciate and decipher the many nuances of Brother-speak.

- ◆ **SHOW VERSUS TELL.** Chances are, your man is not overflowing with emotional expression. Most black men aren't. You can hear the words "I love you," but do yourself and your man a favor: Open your eyes and watch for his display of those words as well. You know what I'm talking about—the little things. The way he rubs your feet, even when they're ashy and crusty. The way he tolerates some of the most obnoxious members of your family. Keeping your ears and eyes open to a black man's language means catching all of those warm "I love you's" he's so often sending out.

✦ **CUT TO THE CHASE.** When most of us talk, we have a tendency to go around the back door, as old folks used to say. We sometimes get off to an abstract start, then build up to our point. Meanwhile, brothers scratch their heads, and more often than not they blurt out some seemingly callous remark, like "Where are you going with this?" Men think in very linear, result-oriented patterns. When you go on for twenty minutes about a subject, you lose them. It's not that they're dumb; they're just wired differently. Dr. Ronn Elmore, a Los Angeles psychologist and the author of *How to Love a Black Man,* urges sisters to give a man the destination (what you want him to do) before you take him on the journey (lay on the details).

✦ **WIN THE WAR, NOT THE BATTLE.** I sometimes think some of my best responses to potential upsets in my twelve-year marriage to Glenn are when I've chosen to say nothing at all. Experts agree that we must choose our battles. That means letting some things go. It also means that while open and honest communication is crucial in a relationship, so is knowing how to look for opportunities that foster it—long drives, walks in the park or around bedtime (providing he's not whupped). Don't expect him to give you his full attention in the fourth quarter of the Final Four championship game or when he's trying to fix his motorcycle.

✦ **PRAISE PUBLICLY, PROTEST PRIVATELY.** Men thrive on feelings of accomplishment, getting the job done. Find any success you can think of and brag on your man as often as possible in the presence of others. Conversely, anytime you have even the slightest complaint to register, wait until you get behind closed doors. Nothing demeans him more than being criticized in public. Besides, it puts you more in the position of a scolding mother than an equal partner.

✦ GIVE HIM TIME. Most of us sisters are fairly in touch with our feelings. When we're hurt or angry, we usually know from whence it came. Brothers are different. They need time to sort such things out. He's not responding as you attempt to explain your pain because he's busy processing—not because he's ignoring you. Don't get mad if right after a confrontation he says he's got to run to the gym or wash the car. Elmore says that 99 percent of him is working through the problem just discussed.

✦ ASK PERMISSION. Before you launch into your opinion on a subject (especially a sensitive one), ask, "Can I offer a suggestion about such and such?" Then proceed only if the answer is yes. Many of us sisters will blurt out our opinions, thinking that since we mean well, our advice will be taken in kind. Nothing could be further from the truth. Often a brother will feel that you're attacking him or demonstrating a lack of faith in his abilities to sort out his own troubles.

✦ TELL IT. Ever think to yourself, "If he really loved me, he would know . . ."? Well, stop right there. I know I've had to stop myself many a time. You have to *tell* a brother what you want, and you have to *tell* him what you need—directly, not by hinting or throwing some psychic vibes. If he leaves his socks on the bathroom floor, say, "Please pick your socks up off of the floor. When you leave them and walk away, I feel like you don't value my time and just expect me to pick them up." This is much more effective than calling him a slob and going on a riff about how you're not a maid.

✦ **FORGIVE AND MOVE ON.** A lot of times we might find that even when we try to approach a subject in neutral tones, our words are tinged with anger. That may be because we're living inside a past experience, one in which our man has let us down. It's crucial to the life of your relationship to deal with anger and hurt feelings quickly and resolutely. Forgiveness is an emotional state that frees us from resentment and fear. Like a lot of sisters, you may associate forgiveness with letting your man off the hook. But ultimately, forgiveness is about letting go. You want to release yourself from the burdensome drain of carrying around negativity and allowing it to taint your attitude.

✦ **DON'T FORGET THAT TOUCHY-FEELY THING.** Remember the matriarchal model. A little tenderness goes a long way. Kiss your man hello and good-bye. Reach for his hand when you walk down the street. This way, even when you have to say something he may not want to hear, he can feel confident that your remarks are coming from a loving place.

From This Day Forward

Meeting your ideal man, courting, becoming engaged, and getting married are all tremendous highs. Each phase takes some work and dedication. But it is after the wedding—when the guests go home and you take off your princess dress—that the real work begins. And trust me, love is not enough to see you through the challenges your marriage will endure. The actress Ruby Dee has said, "One marries many times at many levels within a marriage. If you have more marriages than divorces within the marriage, you're lucky." She must know something about the subject; she's been married to the dashing Ossie Davis for more than fifty years. How can we be assured that our own unions will stand the test of time? Well, certainly there are no guarantees. The average marriage in America lasts only about nine years, but then again, *you're* not an average person.

You should know from jump street, though, that your marriage will not be an endless honeymoon. I find that even couples who've dated exclusively for a long time or lived together for a spell are sometimes surprised to find out how much marriage differs from their expectations. Some sisters labor under the misguided belief that marriage brings two people together, that somehow once you've taken your vows, you become one. Don't fool yourself. Your marriage is simply the start of another journey. And as you set out on that journey, commitment, communication, and compassion will indeed draw you two closer. But not overnight.

Your love and compassion for a brother is what enables you to empathize with him and his struggles. When you truly practice compassion in your marriage, it allows you to be selfless at times for the benefit of the relationship. This is not to be confused with martyrdom. Compassion doesn't mean that you ignore a situation; it means that you choose when to address it based on what seems best for the emotional well-being of your man and the health of the marriage. Simply put, it involves the understanding that your marriage is greater than the sum of its parts.

Communication is something we've talked about over and over in this chapter. But there can never be too much of it. People should not assume that once they reach the point of marriage, the struggle to communicate diminishes in any way. In fact, it may grow more complex. Many brothers harbor a deep and abiding fear of marriage. Society has told them that it makes a woman change, that she will somehow change him. So just when you think you've gotten to the heart of your man's psyche, you two jump the broom and whole new sets of fears rear their heads.

Don't sleep on this major C word; your marital life depends on communication.

When your compassion level seems to be sliding toward "empty" and, despite your best efforts, communication lines are temporarily jammed, what keeps you in there plugging? It may be sex, it may be money, or it may be some other creature comfort. But trust me, those, too, will fade. In a marriage that two people genuinely cherish, it's their commitment to each other that keeps them from walking when times get tough. When you're committed to your man's personal growth and to the marriage itself, you stay and work things through. Unlike with other relationships, the decision becomes not "Should I stay or should I go?" but "How do I make it better?"

Marriages go through cycles, just as your life does. There are up cycles, such as having a baby or buying a home, and down cycles, such as losing a parent or going through a major career change. Both the ups and downs of marriage include stress. As these cycles take place within your relationship, it's important to keep in mind that just because you're soul mates, it's not as though every experience is about both of you. You are indeed a team. But you're also individuals, individuals who've agreed to come together to share a life. What this means is that there will be times when you may be somewhat distant from one another. During such times it becomes important to practice spiritual love and have the courage to let yourself (or your partner) have room to grow.

Fight the Good Fight

Disagreeing is integral to any loving, honest, and mutually respectful marriage. Contrary to the fairy tale some of us buy in to at the beginning of relationships, conflict is not something to be afraid of or avoided. If you and your man aren't fighting, something's wrong. Conflict and tension are a necessary part of growth, and it is through conflict that we learn deep truths about ourselves and each other. The trick is knowing how to fight. Hint: If you're calling him out of his name, yelling over him while he's trying to talk, interrupting, or bringing his mama, his kids, or other family members into the fray, you don't know how to fight productively. See, there are both *de*structive and *in*structive ways to settle our differences. When disputes become more about petty games of tit-for-tat and one-upmanship than about resolving important issues in a marriage, fighting is no longer healthy but destructive. Don't look at fights between you and your man as an opportunity to prove yourself right and him wrong. If you're a sister who thinks fighting is a game of win, lose, or draw, you ought to consider the words of sister-rapper Lauryn Hill, who says, "You may have won, but you really lost one."

In the context of a loving marriage, fighting should be a win-win proposition, where both you and your man come away with a new perspective and a workable solution to a relationship challenge. If you fight the right way—that is, without the intent to hurt or demoralize, but rather to increase understanding—both you and your man can come away feeling all the better for the argument.

Most of us did not grow up with a model of fair fighting. Don't stress it. You can create your own. These are the three basic ground rules:

◆ **KNOW WHAT YOU'RE FIGHTING FOR.** Sometimes we tend to nurse old wounds and use minor pet peeves as surrogate fights. This happens when, for example, you find yourself feeling disrespected or undervalued, but you end up getting on your man about the empty beer cans he and his buddies left out all night. Get your feelings straight and deal with what's really on your mind.

✦ **AVOID GOING INTO BATTLE IN THE HEAT OF A MOMENT.**
Take five, count to ten, or do whatever you need to do to calm
yourself. In order to make a fight constructive rather than
destructive, you'll want to have your wits about you. An emotional tirade will only lead to a confusing bout of flying accu-
sations and hurtful words.

✦ **STICK TO THE POINT.** This is a tough one for me, but it's very
important to master. If you're upset because he didn't call to
tell you he'd be late coming home, argue about that and only
that. You don't need to muddy the waters by bringing up all
the times he's kept you waiting in the past.

Fair fighting is a choice you both should make. However, as
we all know, you can't control the actions of anyone but yourself.
So resolve to follow the guidelines of fairness even when your
man doesn't. And don't hesitate to take the lead in an argument if
it is getting out of hand, by saying something like "We need to talk
about this when we can approach it calmly and rationally. This
isn't getting us anywhere."

There are some elements of productive fighting that need particular attention. These are the things that we often say or do,
without thinking, that send brothers up the wall and quickly
squash any hope of conflict resolution. Here is a brief rundown of
those do's and don'ts:

✦ **BAN "YOU ALWAYS" AND "YOU NEVER" FROM YOUR
VOCABULARY.** First of all, it's highly unlikely that he *always* or
never does anything. And using such phrases will immediately
set off your man's defenses. Instead, use statements that
begin with "I" rather than "you." For example, say "I felt so
lonely when you were talking to your co-workers so much at

the party" instead of "You always leave me stranded; you know I didn't know any of those people." The emphasis should be on how his actions made *you* feel. The latter statement will make him feel attacked.

✦ **DON'T FORGET THE IMPORTANCE OF BODY LANGUAGE.** It should go without saying, but finger pointing, neck bobbing, and hip shaking are a sure way to incite a black man's ire. You're his woman, not his mother. Remember that you're discussing a problem, not reprimanding mischievous behavior.

✦ **DON'T MISS WHAT YOUR MAN IS SAYING.** Too often we have a tendency to "listen" only as a way to formulate our next response. Even though he may not fire off his feelings as quickly as you do, don't finish his sentences or rush his thoughts. Once he has finished, follow up with your interpretation of what's been said: "So I hear you saying that you feel . . . Is that right?"

✦ **DON'T THREATEN.** If you say things like "If you don't shape up, I'm leaving," after a while these kinds of words will take root and destroy any fiber of trust. Dissolving a marriage is serious, and to trivialize it by throwing threats into every conflict is a disservice to the sanctity of your vows.

Keep It Hot — Twenty Ways

By nurturing your relationship with those three Cs—compassion, communication, and commitment—you can't help but keep it real. But if the passion is to continue burning alive, you've also got to keep it hot. In the early days of a union it's difficult to fathom that the sexing and romancing will ever end. But as real life begins to intrude, you will see that some days your love machine looks as though he's running out of steam. Here are twenty ways to help put the pep back into his step—and yours.

1. Kiss him passionately (when you're not having sex) at least three times a day.

2. Leave love notes in his car, on the bathroom mirror, or in his briefcase.

3. Say "I love you" once a day—at least.

4. Celebrate your love each month (perhaps on the date of your first kiss) with a special night of lovemaking.

5. Plan a romantic getaway for a day or weekend.

6. Establish a weekly or biweekly date night, whether it's dinner and a movie or just a cup of coffee.

7. Surprise him with sexy new lingerie on a weeknight.

8. Take a bath together with candles and scented oils.

9. Go out dancing, or put some good slow drag tunes in the CD player and dance at home.

10. Take a walk on the beach.

11. Call him at work just to say "I miss you."

12. Mail him a romantic greeting card.

13. Read an erotic book or watch a sexy movie together.

14. Give him a massage.

15. Send him flowers.

16. Make having sex a choice; if you simply wait for the mood to strike, you can sometimes go weeks without loving.

17. At bedtime, spoon him by snuggling up close as you both lie on your sides.

18. Once a day tell your man something you appreciate about him.

19. Send him a sexy e-mail message.

20. Surprise him with a "quickie" sex session on a weekday morning.

Chapter 7

LOOKING GOOD,
FEELING GREAT

STYLE DIRECTOR, *ESSENCE MAGAZINE*. That's how my business cards read back in 1995. For any sister-journalist on the fashion scene, this was the bomb assignment. I mean, I was the anointed arbiter of sister chic, the embodiment of black women's style.

But with this career high came some unexpected lows in terms of my own self-image. After years of neglect, my naturally voluptuous size-twelve frame had ballooned to an untoned eighteen. Many of the hottest styles of the day—cropped and fitted tops, slim and hip-skimming slacks, and barely-there slip dresses— would only serve to exaggerate the figure flaws I wanted to hide.

And even if I could squeeze into the sexy new fashions, I wasn't trying to be fashion-fabulous at the expense of a depleted bank account. I'd never been one to wear my salary on my back. I pride myself on being able to create the "in" look at an affordable price. But in the fashion world, those with whom I did business daily knew a designer outfit when they saw one—*and* they knew if it was from last season. Both mattered.

Of course, some of my counterparts from big fashion magazines had wardrobe expense accounts. Not I. Others, at the very least, had size-eight bodies that allowed them to wear the clothes many designers gave them for little or nothing. At this point, especially, I was in no way willing or able to pour my money into a wardrobe of trendy designer clothes. My bed-and-breakfast, Akwaaba Mansion, was just getting off the ground, and I was trying to build on its success with the purchase of a building to launch a fine restaurant. I may have wanted the Guccis and Calvins, but I needed the Benjamins for bricks.

As a result, even though I knew fashion like the back of my hand—I had spent nearly fifteen years at Fairchild Publications, the company behind *W* and the fashion bible *Women's Wear Daily*—I rose from bed each morning with a gnawing in the pit of my stomach. There were two things at issue: Deep inside, I felt like a fraud. By encouraging millions of sisters to do what I myself would not—drop hundreds of dollars on the latest must-have of the season—I was frontin'. My other problem was far less esoteric and, on a certain level, far more deflating. I didn't *look* like the style director of *Essence*. I was reminded of the fact every time I waded through my closet in search of an outfit that would both enhance my credentials as the black woman's fashion editrix and flatter my ample physique.

I'm not going to lie; it messed with me. It worked my confidence and played on my self-image like few experiences before or since.

The Wake-up Call

Beyond not fully embracing the body I saw in the mirror, I knew that my current lifestyle of no exercise and late-night, fast-food eating put me on a dangerous course. And I know I'm not the only one. As a people, we sisters and brothers are in the midst of a national health crisis. One out of every three of us lives with high blood pressure. One in ten suffers from diabetes. And because we often delay our doctor visits and don't have the means to seek aggressive treatment, if we get cancer, only half of us survive.

According to the U.S. Department of Commerce Economic and Statistics Administrative Bureau of the Census, our life expectancies fall far short of our white counterparts'. While white American men can enjoy a life span of about seventy-six years, our brothers can expect to die at about age sixty-five. White women will live six years after most sisters pass away at about seventy-four.

I certainly did not want to become another statistic. And in 1998 I got a direct, person-to-person, you're-the-one wake-up call. My younger brother, Donald, was stricken with a heart attack at age thirty-five. My father and my thirty-two-year-old "baby" sister were living with sugar diabetes, and my mother was suffering with heart disease and high blood pressure. I knew I had to do something. I hired a personal trainer.

Now, let me tell you, for someone like me, this was drastic. I was never one of those sisters to be found bouncing up and down at a health club. I didn't know Nautilus or his brother Cybex, and I wasn't trying to get acquainted. To my mind, teeny beads of sweat running across my forehead could be the result of only one of two things: a funky good time on the dance floor or a rousing and romantic night of passion with my husband, Glenn. And thanks to my hectic pace, my body wasn't experiencing either one of those as often as I would've liked.

Getting Fit

I knew that my very life depended on making a change, and change I did. At six every other morning, my trainer, Duvall, arrives at my door. In the beginning I woke up at five-thirty for him. Being a "good girl," never wanting to disappoint, I figured he had gotten up for me so I owed it to him. Besides, I was spending money that I really didn't have for this trainer. But I was finally getting the message: I'm worth it! Soon after, I got up just for me and worked out at the crack of dawn even if I had stayed in the office till midnight the night before. I figured out that exercising was the only thing in my life that I do strictly for me. I decided to cheat myself no longer.

I work out in the morning because it's the time I'm least likely to be interrupted. Some people like to exercise at lunchtime, because it gives them a much-needed energy boost. Still others do it after work. When you decide to work your body is up to you; the important thing is "you better work it."

Always consult your medical doctor before taking on a strenuous exercise regimen for the first time. Most people start their session with a cardio or aerobic activity—a brisk walk, run, bike ride—any vigorous movement that gets your heart really pumping for at least thirty minutes. I like power-walking fourteen laps around the track at the local high school. I'm inspired by the seniors who come there each morning to get their blood circulating, and when some pretty young thang whizzes by me on the track, I'm encouraged to pep up my step. I never run, though. I'm concerned about the impact running would have on my knees, and a brisk walk can burn almost as many calories as jogging. Next, I incorporate a strength-training routine. This means lifting weights or doing some resistance moves. Contrary to common sister-think, lifting a few light weights will not—I repeat, *not*—

cause your thigh muscles to bulge like those of the macho-looking women you sometimes see on the covers of body-building magazines. What it will do is help tighten that sexy strut, leaving you a rearview with more sizzle and less jiggle. My local YMCA has all the equipment I need for a solid workout—and membership is only $250 a year.

Following are a few tips that put me on the road to fitness:

+ **LOOK THE PART** by wearing shorts or roomy sweats. Comfort, not diva fashion, is the key here.

+ **START SMALL** with a workout you can master. Your success will inspire you to take the next step.

+ **COUNT BACKWARD** when doing repetitions, say, one hundred sit-ups. Psychologically, it makes the task more bearable.

+ **PACE YOURSELF** with someone in the gym or on the field who is slightly further along than you.

+ **COMPLETE THE TASK TO FAILURE** even if you feel you can't reach the desired goal. Don't say "I can't" before you try.

+ **INCREASE YOUR PROGRAM GRADUALLY AND REGULARLY.** If you don't constantly challenge your body to reach the next peak, it will become accustomed to the routine and yield little result. Progressive resistance is the name of the game.

+ **CHANGE IT UP SO YOU DON'T GET BORED.** If you usually walk the treadmill, try a neighborhood walk for variety. Better yet, try bike riding.

+ **ALTERNATE THE BODY PARTS YOU WORK,** allowing a day or so for recovery.

+ **GET AN EXERCISE BUDDY,** whether it's a trainer you pay or a girlfriend who's on the same mission. A partner will help motivate you when you're having trouble doing it for yourself.

After four decades of living, I am probably in the best shape of my life. My muscles are toned. The roundness of my curves has begun to firm. And for the first time I think I get what people mean when they talk about exercise as a mind-body connection. I feel rejuvenated and confident—not to mention proud that I'm making the effort.

Eating Right

Of course, all that working out means very little if you load up on all the calories and fat you're trying to burn off. I've learned to view food completely differently. Instead of living to eat, I eat to live. Fortunately, I had eliminated pork and red meat from my diet in the late eighties, when my husband refused to kiss me after I had a nice, juicy pork chop. He knew early on that pork and too much red meat can lead to high cholesterol and clogging of the arteries. A high-fat diet has also been linked to certain forms of cancer.

My greatest weaknesses are sweets and fatty fried foods. I still struggle to resist a danish or an overgrown muffin in the morning with my tea, and the task is even harder now that we own a coffeehouse, where pastries sit on doily-covered plates just waiting for me. When I started my fitness routine with Duvall, there were some basic—though trying—dietary rules:

✦ **CUT DOWN ON CARBOHYDRATES.** (You know, breads, potatoes, pasta—AKA macaroni and cheese). A diet rich in carbs, especially made from processed or enriched grains, bloats the body and increases your blood sugar. The body processes fruits, vegetables, and protein more efficiently.

✦ **DRINK A MINIMUM OF EIGHT GLASSES OF WATER DAILY.** Water flushes your system. I simply keep two thirty-two-ounce bottles of water at my desk each day and drink from them regularly.

✦ **ALWAYS EAT BEFORE A WORKOUT.** "You wouldn't—or couldn't—drive your car without gas," Duvall always says. While I understand the reasoning, getting up any earlier than five-thirty just to eat is truly extra. And then there was the dilemma of what to eat. Pancakes, two scrambled eggs on a roll, a muffin at the very least had been my lifelong breakfast options. Now, because I was cutting way back on carbs, I was forced to be creative at the crack of dawn. Tuna with a piece of fruit fast became my new A.M. special.

✦ **DON'T SKIP MEALS.** In all the years I've dieted, I always thought that eating less was a good thing. When I did Weight Watchers, I was diligent about weighing my food so as not to eat too much. Now I was being told to eat often; otherwise my body would think I was starving it and would store any food I finally did eat rather than breaking it down and releasing it. The key is to eat the right foods regularly—lean chicken or fish, either baked or grilled; fresh fruit; steamed vegetables; and salad with nonfat dressing.

✦ **CHEAT SMART.** If you're going to stray from what you know is right, be strategic. An individual-size bag of caramel-covered popcorn—my favorite cheat snack—is only about 110 calories, and no fat!

The Beauty Stealers

You can eat right and exercise regularly, but you still must beware of the natural beauty stealers. I'm talking about those culprits like lack of rest and the "party" life. They rob our eyes of their sparkle, our skin of its radiance and our hair of its brilliance and shine. Now more than ever, black women as a group must take care of ourselves so that we can do the critical work of raising our families and building our communities. *Essence* beauty director Mikki Taylor often reminds me about a passage from the Bible. In 1 Corinthians 3:16–17, we learn that our bodies are temples of God, and it is within our bodies that the Spirit of the living God dwells. Your body, then, is holy—just as the temple of God is holy. It is inherently filled with divine power. On some level of our psyche, most of us know this. Yet we can sometimes mistreat or neglect our bodies in very unholy ways—drinking, smoking, overeating, taking illicit drugs. And believe me, not even the best makeup can cover up a hangover.

Many of us treat our cars better than we treat our own bodies, which is a shame, because an automobile can at least be traded in for a newer, sleeker version. The body God gave you, on the other hand, is not a demo or test model. And what you put into it is ultimately what you will get out of it. Yet we take our body for granted. We expect it to make long hauls on minimum or sub-quality fuel, like sugar and caffeine. We allow its engine to become sluggish from exhaustion (we really do need close to seven hours of sleep a night). And worse, most of us rarely take the time to have our body checked or serviced. Think of regular medical appointments as the oil and lube job your body needs every thousand miles or so to maintain peak performance.

The Beauty Enhancers

Just as there are natural beauty stealers, there are beauty enhancers. If you look in the mirror and love what you see—flawless complexion, happening hair, features any camera would love—God bless you. But if, like me, what you see is passable but improvable, read on.

The key to putting your best face forward is proper skin care. There's only so much that makeup can do. As a group, we sisters are blessed. Our skin has more melanin or pigment in it than that of white women, which means, to a certain extent, we have a built-in defense against harsh elements like the sun. You very rarely see a sister in her early thirties with fine lines around her eyes and mouth. But before you go getting cocky, remember: Good skin doesn't just happen. Even if you possess a smooth, even complexion, you must work to maintain its glow. So establish a routine that includes cleansing, exfoliating, moisturizing, and an occasional facial.

If you've learned one thing about me so far, you know I'm into simple. So here's what I do: wash, tone, and moisturize twice daily with Black Opal's skin-care products. Each week I give myself a mini-facial by exfoliating and applying a mask. It works for me. This book is about helping you find out what works for you. By sharing what I've gleaned from two decades in the fashion and beauty business, I can shorten your learning curve. In the end, however, it's about you playing around a little to find the products that suit your style and budget. What follows are the basics.

Determine your skin type and select products that enhance it:

♦   DRY SKIN feels tight and rough to the touch, and visible dry patches may be present in certain areas. Avoid harsh soaps and moisturize, moisturize, moisturize.

- **VERY DRY OR SENSITIVE SKIN** is prone to discomfort and extreme tightness; many products irritate the face. Creamy cleansers are preferable to soaps.

- **COMBINATION SKIN** is both oily and dry, depending on the area; usually forehead, nose, and chin are shiny and oily, the other areas dry. Apply astringents and toners to oily "T-zone" areas only.

- **OILY SKIN** breaks out, and blemishes occur often; pores are enlarged, and shine is virtually never-ending. Cleanse regularly, and use moisturizers on an as-needed basis.

Use products that are formulated to work with your particular skin type. But be aware, these are just the main categories. You may have skin that feels tight and looks shiny, or your dry skin may be prone to pimples. Trouble skin often needs professional attention. Don't hesitate to see a dermatologist if you are having difficulty finding a skin-care regimen that complements your skin type.

The Skin Commandments

Thou Shalt Not:

1. Squeeze or pick pimples.

2. Smoke.

3. Put makeup on an unwashed face.

4. Go to sleep with makeup on.

5. Strip the skin by overcleansing.

6. Use products that are not made for your skin type.

7. Skimp on sunscreen.

8. Put fade products all over the face—instead of limiting them to dark spots.

9. Use unwashed makeup sponges or a friend's tools.

10. Ignore product instructions.

Now that your skin is luminous and healthy, you're ready to apply the final touch—makeup. Culturally, we are a people rich with pride, and ritualistic personal adornment is one of our oldest expressions of that pride. Some of us love makeup. Some of us hate it. But I'll be blunt. All of us can benefit from at least a little bit of it.

I like to think of makeup as the quintessential accessory. But there's a difference between wearing makeup and letting makeup wear you. Knowing how to apply makeup—with a deft and light hand—is what makes that difference.

Let me begin by telling you that as drop-dead gorgeous as *Essence* cover subjects are, not one camera is clicked before each undergoes hours of hair and makeup. You've seen *Essence*'s covers, so you know that time is well spent. But you and I don't have a staff of pros working on us daily, and we're not getting paid for our looks. Yet we want to look good—damn good, even—in ten minutes or less. Most days my face routine takes about five minutes. I keep my brows shaped—they really define the face—and I brush on some mascara, stroke on some lipstick, and blot on some powder for shine control. I'm here to tell you, from Oprah Winfrey to Halle Berry, Queen Latifah to Tyra Banks—faces that couldn't be more beautiful or diverse—they all undergo the same basic routines. The following are the must-have elements of good face, in order of importance: a well-groomed brow, foundation or powder, lipstick, blush, and mascara.

Brow Know-how

Framing the most important feature on your face—the eyes—is more than a mere notion. The shape and texture of your eyebrow will help define your entire face. Lots of sisters—myself included—prefer to hand over the delicate task of arching eyebrows to the professionals. You can visit a hair or nail salon in most cities and have your brows waxed or tweezed for around ten to fifteen dollars. You can also do it well yourself with the help of a brow kit, which includes a stencil so you know where to remove hair and where to fill in with a brow pencil.

Whatever you do, don't try to mimic the brow line of your best friend or someone you saw in a magazine because you think it's fly. You can no sooner bite your neighbor's brow shape than you can copy her personality. A good brow shaping should enhance your own face's shape and contours. To determine your natural brow line, place the bottom of a pencil vertically alongside your right nostril. Your brow should not extend beyond the pencil. Then, swing the pencil clockwise so it aligns with the outside corner of your eye. That's where your brow should end. Finally, look straight ahead and place the pencil in front of your face slightly to the outside of your iris. Right here is where your brow should arch subtly.

Lip Service

Lipstick, in my opinion, is probably the most important makeup product you can buy. It evens out the natural shade of your lips and adds color, moisture, and shine. If you have to run out of the house in a hurry, lipstick will at least bring some nice color to your face.

Buying it: There is a maddening array of colors available, and lipstick comes in just about every form you can imagine—from matte to gloss, tubes to pencil-like crayons. Drugstore brands are, of course, less than half the cost of department store lines, and at about five dollars a tube, most women can afford to buy as many as their heart desires. The goal, however, is to have the *right* shades—not just a dozen different shades. As is the case with most makeup on the market, we sisters are likely to fare better by going with a line made especially with our skin tones in mind. Otherwise, if you choose a light color, it could end up looking pretty pasty, and if you want to go with a dark shade, it may lack the richness you need. Seek out the help of a professional; visit a department store and ask the person at the makeup counter which shades are best for your complexion. For me, it's also important to have long-lasting color; I'm not one to apply and reapply makeup throughout the day. I just get too busy. Years ago, many of the all-day formulations felt harsh and dry on the lips, but most cosmetics companies have now perfected the product, making it possible to select from creamy, nondrying textures in an array of shades that stay on all day.

Applying it: Just follow your natural lip line, smack your kissers together, and blot with a tissue. This last step is one many women omit, but if you want your lipstick to look like natural color, not a fresh coat of super-high-gloss paint, the tissue-blotting trick is very important. Lining the lip goes in and out of vogue, it seems. I don't do it, to be honest. I have a natural line, and I don't see a need to add any unnecessary steps. If you do choose to line, make sure you use a liner close to the lipstick shade you're wearing that day. Superdark pencil rimmed around a light shade of lip color is *not* the move. It looks hard and way too deliberate.

Good Foundations

As the name indicates, foundation should be the staring point for your makeup routine. It is used as a base to even out your skin tone, fill in fine lines, and mask blemishes and other imperfections. It can be bought in the form of a liquid, a cake, or a stick, depending on how much coverage you need. It's usually best to opt for the kind of sheer, all-over coverage liquids provide. Cake and stick formulations are typically reserved for theatrical use, because they come off heavy and masklike. Several manufacturers offer something called dual-finish foundation. It looks like a powder, comes in a compact case, and can be used with a wet or dry sponge applicator.

Buying it: It's imperative that your foundation matches your skin tone. This is not easy for us sisters, because cosmetics companies don't always offer an assortment of shades to fit our kaleidoscopic range of beige to honey to chocolate hues. Finding the right foundation may mean spending more time and more money on the purchase, especially if you have to have it custom-blended. But this is the one makeup product that's worth it. It's also the cosmetic purchase where—more than any other—you can truly benefit from expert advice. I suggest you visit a few beauty emporiums or department store makeup counters. It doesn't cost anything to ask questions. Don't buy any shade without trying it on your face—none of this back-of-the-hand business. Your hands and face are usually not exactly the same color. In most department stores the lighting is nowhere close to natural. So even if the salesperson has to come with you, take a small mirror outside to check the foundation without the glare of fluorescent light.

Applying it: The best way to put on your foundation is with a wedged makeup sponge. You can buy a bunch of these inexpensively in any drugstore. Start with clean, dry hands. Wet the sponge, making sure to squeeze out excess water. Put a small amount of foundation in the palm of your hand, then dip the sponge. Start out with small areas first. Many women make the mistake of applying makeup to places like the forehead and cheeks, then working inward. The result is usually a telltale makeup line. You want to begin around the eyes, nose, and lips, then work outward. This way there's less makeup in those harder-to-blend areas such as the hairline and neck. It's advisable to set the foundation with a loose powder.

Shadow Dancing

Eye shadow is a good way to define and add color to your eyes. Available in every form from powder to pencil to cream, it also comes in as many colors as you can imagine. But don't be fooled by the allure of those beautiful azure and ocher shades. The truth is, there are only a handful of hues that will really work well for you. So while those huge trays often sold as gift sets at your local department store may look like a bargain, you'll save money (not to mention drawer space) by concentrating on three or four of your best colors.

Many fashion and beauty magazines go for fantasy. Their objective is to capture the reader's attention and imagination, but the look is not intended to be wearable. Nevertheless, I've seen women walking down the street mocking a beauty layout. Like dangerous TV stunts, those magazines ought to run a warning under each caption: DON'T TRY THIS AT HOME. Instead, pick warm, earthy shades—russet, eggplant, coffee—and you'll rarely go wrong.

Buying it: First decide what form of shadow you can work with best. Generally, powders look more natural and blend more smoothly. Creams and pencils give off a shiny finish and require a more experienced hand. Again, visit the cosmetics counter at your local department store and have a professional application. This way you can get a good idea of the colors that suit you and where on your lid you should apply them. Ask that the counter person give you a look for day as well as evening. If you like the results, find out if you can purchase all the colors packaged together. This will be cheaper than buying each shade individually. Eye shadow isn't too expensive, and once you determine the type and colors that appeal to you, there's no need to be especially brand-loyal.

Applying it: Always put on your eye shadow before you apply eyeliner or mascara. You can apply it any one of several ways: with a sponge-tip applicator, a makeup wedge, or an eye shadow brush. A sponge-tip, which most manufacturers package with the shadow itself, gives you the heaviest coverage and perhaps the least control. Brushes will give you the lightest coating.

If you've done your homework, I know you already have the skills down pat on where to place colors to optimize your eye shape and contours. So the only thing I can tell you is practice as much as you can. It seems tricky I know, but the more you try it, the sooner you'll master the winning techniques.

Blushing Beauty

The purpose of blush is to add color and definition to cheeks. You can buy it in powder, liquid, or cream form. Have you ever seen a woman walking around with two perfectly rouged circles drawn on her cheeks? We don't want that. Creams and liquids can give you that dewy look, but only if you're a makeup artist or really, really know what you're doing. Most of us layfolk are better off with powder blush.

Buying it: Color is everything. It should always be a soft, subtle tone that highlights your complexion. You can pick up a shade at any drugstore or five-and-dime, but I wouldn't advise it until you've gone to a department store and played with the samples. Again, remember to check the shade in natural lighting.

Blush is not easy for most of us sisters to buy. The dark-skinned among us usually want to go with something in a brownish-rosy family. But it depends on your skin's undertones. Some of us have more yellow in our skin; others have more red or blue. The bluer your skin tone, the browner you want your blusher. Yellow undertones warm best to reds and coppers. Even if you're light-skinned, blush can be problematic. A lot of the soft shades make us look pasty or ashy. My advice here is to seek out the brands formulated with us in mind.

Applying it: Almost all blush is packaged with dinky little brushes. You may as well toss them in the trash. Apply your blush with a large brush, using big sweeping strokes from your cheek-bones to your hairline. Blush is not something you want people to notice. It should be the makeup product you use most sparingly in your routine.

Smashing Lashes

Mascara coats and defines your eyelashes. It takes only a minute to apply, but for my money, a few strokes, coupled with lip color, pack the biggest impact when it comes to great face.

Buying it: Nowadays mascara comes in a wide variety of colors. In my experience, violet and other shades are fine for a photo shoot or an extra-special evening look. But blacks and browns have the prettiest, most natural effect for daytime against our skin tones. You can buy mascara in a variety of formulations, including waterproof, water-soluble, and with added moisturizers and such. All you really need is one that goes on smoothly—you know, no clumping or smudging. And there are many cheap, drugstore brands that perform just as well as the expensive, prestige lines.

Applying it: You should apply mascara with the applicator it's packaged with. Stroke it onto your top lashes in upward motions. Don't apply mascara to the lower lashes. It can make you look "made up," and usually it smears on the skin, causing raccoon-eye circles. If you botch your mascara or happen to sneeze in the middle of applying it as I often do, just take a cotton swab dipped in makeup remover and wipe it off.

Mane Event

If you're like most sisters, at various times your hair has probably been your best friend and your worst enemy. When it's right, no one can tell you a thing. You know you've got it going on. But when your hair looks bad, it's almost like having sore feet—everything is wrong. You don't feel like smiling, and even your flyest outfit stops working.

Fortunately, I think we've gotten somewhat past the "bad hair/good hair" days when the standard of beauty was naturally smooth, wavy tendrils. Today we sisters have come to terms with our hair, whether natural or relaxed, in all of its myriad textures, lengths, and styles.

I for one have just about done it all. For years I relaxed my hair and sported bobs and other smooth dos, convinced that it was the only way to achieve a polished, professional look. Then one day, while on vacation in the British Virgin Islands, I decided to take it all off. My permed hair was all over my head from the heat and humidity. And in the cottage room right next door to me was Peggy Dillard, the legendary beauty who distinguished herself in the eighties as a cover model without ever having straightened her hair, which was de rigueur back then. I watched her pull her natural hair up into a flirty Afro-puff-like do one day and on the next day wear it in a freeform 'fro. Then, on the following day, she parted it into sections and sported Bantu knots. It didn't take much for Peggy, who at that time owned the popular New York natural hair salon Turning Heads, to convince me to let her cut my hair. I liked the idea of going back to my nappy roots, even though I was a little apprehensive about really short hair because I'd never had it before. But even more, I wanted the ease of a low-maintenance style. That was in 1996. Since then I've gone from a neat, short 'fro to a shoulder-grazing natural style that has given me more ease and versatility than ever. Sometimes I twist it. Other times I undo the twists and let it hang carefree. And then there are days when I gather it into an upswept style—just like Peggy.

Keep It Manageable

However you choose to wear your hair, the most important thing you can do is keep it healthy and strong. Not only will your hair look good, it will be easier to manage and style. There are all kinds of products on the market designed to make your hair look healthy—from sheen sprays to gels and pomades. There's certainly nothing wrong with giving hair a little boost, but the fact is, most of these products are simply too little too late. What determines how your hair looks is the health of your cuticle.

The cuticle is what coats the outside shell of each hair shaft. And everything you do to your hair, including washing, brushing, blow-drying, coloring, or perming—can chip away at the cuticle. If it becomes damaged, your hair will look dry and dull. While conditioners and other products can help it look better, there's really nothing you can do to repair a damaged shaft. So the trick is not to ruin it in the first place. Wash, dry, and brush your hair gently, and use chemicals cautiously and preferably only under the care of a qualified professional. If you wear a weave, be especially concerned about how your hairstylist attaches it. Some of the waxy glues used in the bonding process for weaves actually pull out your own hair when you go to take out the added-on hair. Likewise, if you braid your hair or wear extensions, you run the risk of breaking the hair at the hairline by pulling it too tightly. This is called "tension alopecia" (alopecia means hair loss), and it's a high price to pay for a stylish do.

Keep It Simple

Few things work against a woman's credibility like silly hair. I'm sorry. I know I shouldn't be judgmental, but when I see hair that's teased and piled a foot high atop a sister's head with a maze of curls and swirls in the middle of the day, "silly" is the only word that comes to mind.

Hair that is done up in such a dramatic fashion probably brings just the opposite of the effect you may be after; it calls attention not to you but to your hair. It detracts from your gorgeous face, your slamming body—everything. Complicated braids, hard finger waves, and sky-high chignons might be appropriate for a dramatic evening look, but your everyday style should be simple and easy to understand.

Grooming Matters

✦ **NAIL POWER.** I know a lot of sisters wouldn't be caught dead without their nails tipped and polished to perfection. If that's you, I say more power to you. I am not the one. I have too little time to keep up with the special manicures diva nails require. All one really needs to look polished is clean, well-groomed hands. I'm talking about a set of ten, neatly trimmed fingernails of uniform length and free of dry, overhanging cuticles. I especially like to buff my nails to a brilliant shine, or I have the manicurist apply a coat of clear polish or one of the simple, sheer pastel shades commonly used for French manicures. That way if the polish starts to chip before I can make it back to the nail salon, it's not as unsightly as chipped red polish would be.

♦ **DASHING ASH.** Picture this: It's a hot summer day, and you're strutting down the street in your sunshine finery. Then, you look down. Yikes! Your elbows look rusty, your heels crusty. You are one ashy sister. How did it happen? You used a moisturizing bath gel this morning. You were slightly rushed, but you did apply some lotion when you stepped out of the shower. It's no secret; our skin is prone to ash, especially in certain areas like knees and elbows. There is a way to dash that ash, but it takes more than a quick once-over with generic body cream. Invest in moisture products that are rich in emollients and made especially for dry or extra-dry skin. There are loads of products available, which is half the fun. Use your daily moisturizing routine as a way to pamper yourself with the healing warmth of touch. When you spot a body cream or lotion high in ingredients like vitamin E, shea, or cocoa butter, take note. These should do the job. If your skin is normal, apply a superenriched product to the problem areas only. In a pinch you can go old-school: Smooth on some all-purpose, fail-safe petroleum jelly. I wouldn't make this a habit, though. Not only will it give a lot more shine than you may have bargained for, when you use it on your feet you may notice that it attracts dirt and dust from the street. However, applying petroleum jelly to your feet at night after a bath or shower, then sleeping in a pair of socks, is a great way to keep your footsies soft, smooth, and crust-free.

✦ **HAIR APPARENT.** You would never think to leave the house with hairy armpits, right? Yet many of us feel it's okay to walk around with other kinds of body and facial hair. I used to be one of those sisters. In the D.C. neighborhood where I came of age, brothers found it sexy to see hair on a woman's legs. Likewise, a light mustache was a turn-on. But take it from me, aside from a few brothers, most people don't find excess hair appealing. If you're going to present yourself to the professional world, leg, facial, and underarm hair removal is just plain good grooming. There is absolutely no truth to the myth that removing the hair will make it grow back thicker. It *is* true that some forms of hair removal leave you prone to hair bumps, especially in the bikini and underarm area. But you can usually avoid that unsightly inconvenience with regular use of a loofah sponge, which gently exfoliates the skin. There are all kinds of ways to remove unwanted hair. Here's the 411 on the various options and the pros and cons of each.

Shaving
PROS: Works everywhere, except lip and chin; inexpensive; relatively pain-free (as long as you don't nick yourself); and removes all types of hair.
CONS: Hair will grow back quickly.

Tweezing
PROS: Good for eyebrows and other facial hair; cheap and relatively easy.
CONS: It stings, and hair grows back quickly.

Waxing
PROS: Good on just about all areas; cheap if done at home, but better left to a salon specialist; hair takes two to four weeks to grow back.

CONS: It hurts; you have to wait till hair grows out at least a quarter inch in order for waxing to take; salon costs can be pricey: ten dollars for eyebrow or underarm and up to sixty dollars for leg and bikini.

Depilatories
PROS: Work well on body and face; the chemicals can remove hair more thoroughly than shaving; cheap to do at home; takes about a week for hair to grow back.
CONS: They can irritate sensitive skin; the chemicals are smelly; don't always work well on coarse or curly hair, so us sisters often end up with uneven results.

Electrolysis
PROS: Works best on small areas, like the chin and upper lip; removes hair permanently.
CONS: At about fifty bucks an hour, it's pricey; it can be very time-consuming—removing hair on a small area can mean many trips to the electrolysis technician to zap all the hairs.

Winning Wardrobe

When I got my first job in New York as a fashion journalist, I was ready. I packed away all that trendy gear that made me one of the best-dressed on Howard's fashionable campus and invested in dress-for-success clothes, just like that John T. Malloy book advised all college graduates to do when entering the "real" world. It was the early eighties, a time when women were coming into their own in the workplace. I packed my suitcase with the kinds of clothes I thought appropriate for the power role I planned to ascend to at Fairchild Publications, a leader among fashion magazine houses. That meant lots of suits, mostly navy or gray, soft blouses, and two-inch-heeled pumps.

I wore this "uniform" proudly and confidently each day, until one morning a female editor I'd grown close to pulled me aside. "You know, Monique," she said, "you could loosen up a bit. At fashion magazines we tend to dress more laid-back and . . . well, fashionably."

I was crushed. I had failed to be cognizant of the unwritten dress code. While what I was wearing would have worked beautifully on Wall Street, it was just plain out of place on Twelfth Street in New York's Greenwich Village. I was grateful that this editor had taken the time to set me straight, and I loosened up, immediately and gladly.

Clothes wield power. Think of the many assumptions we make about each other based on a way of dress. If you'd met me in my power-suit days, you'd likely have considered me rigid, stuck-up, at the very least conformist. Yet I'm none of those things.

Creating Your Personal Style

Dress for success. It sounds like a tired cliché, but trust me as someone who has managed some two hundred–odd employees over the years: Your boss will indeed be impressed to see you show up for work in take-me-seriously clothes. Unless you screw up big time, your attire is not likely to get you fired, but if you dress for the job you aspire to, you're far more likely to be noticed and, thus, promoted. Professionally speaking, you don't want to wear clothes that scream and shout. Your wardrobe should calmly say, "I'm confident and competent, and I command respect."

Study the professional style of those to whom you report. If they wear suits, so should you. I'm not suggesting you break the bank to keep up with people who make at least twice your salary. But I am saying that if it's suits you're going to wear, invest in one or two made of the highest quality your budget will allow. Then mix and match to create coordinated ensembles.

I know better than most that the hot look in fashion changes like the weather. Hemlines go up and down like the stock market. One day Seventh Avenue calls for tough street looks, the next day it's soft and feminine. The fickle winds of fashion will never stop blowing, and if you're intent on following each breeze, you'll only make yourself crazy. So take my advice: Stick with the classics. If you're over fifteen, these are the looks that probably best suit you anyway. Classics endure the whims of the fashion press. And unlike, let's say that orange spandex cat suit in the back of your closet, well-cut classics look good season after season. Accessories are where you can have fun and make a real statement. I often accent my classic business gear with conversation-starting, Afrocentric pieces, like my hand-beaded watchband from South Africa or the spiral cluster bracelet that combines pearls and brass beads with golden ankhs and cowrie shells.

Always consider a few basic truths when perfecting your style: What do I like? What makes me feel pretty? What flatters me? Hint: The last and first are sometimes mutually exclusive.

To Thine Own Self Be True

Self-image is a tricky matter. Most of us like to believe we have a pretty clear picture of ourselves. We get up and dress ourselves based on this vision we have of who we are and what we want to present to the world. Problem is, sometimes this vision is a little cloudy. Some sisters suffer from two common afflictions of the style-challenged: They're either age-impaired or size-deluded. Wearing skirts that are too short, blouses that are too tight, and heels that are too high are some of the surest ways to lose credibility among your peers and your subordinates alike. Unless you're trying to land a spot in a music video or hoping to be chosen from behind the velvet ropes to gain entrance to the latest "in" club, your daywear should not consist of painted-on jeans, hot pants, or underwear worn as outerwear—even if you happen to have the body to pull it off.

The Age-impaired

There are two problems that usually underlie those who are age-impaired. First, such sisters are desperate to be a decade, if not a generation, younger than they really are. Second, they crave the attention that ultrasexy clothes invite. What few realize, however, is that they aren't fooling anyone but themselves, and the attention gained from wearing these getups—gawking stares from men, disapproving whispers from colleagues—is far from positive. Remember what your mama probably told you when you were a little girl coming up: "There's a time and place for everything." If you're over eighteen and trying to build a career for yourself, this is not the time for hottie wear. And if you're working in a professional atmosphere, it is definitely not the place.

The Size-deluded

Some of us have similarly flawed self-images when it comes to proper dress size. Perhaps you were chubby as a child, and despite the fact that you've long shed your baby fat, you still see yourself as overweight. Instead of wearing tailored clothes that flatter, you hide in oversize styles that actually make you appear to be the big girl you once saw in the mirror. Your attempts to hide your perceived figure flaws under yards and yards of fabric have several unintended effects. Baggy, ill-fitting clothes can't help but look sloppy, especially on women who aren't very tall. The shoulders of a garment hang, the waistline droops, and nothing falls well. You may think you're hiding, but what the rest of the world sees is a sister who doesn't care enough about herself to dress neatly.

The flip side is, of course, someone who buys her clothes too small, thinking she'll soon shed the pounds needed to fit into them. In the meantime she wears the skirt that bunches at the hip, the blouse that pulls across the bosom, and the slacks whose pleats can't rest smoothly. No matter if you're squeezing your size-eighteen form into a sixteen or your size-eight body into a six, the world sees a woman who looks uncomfortable in her own skin.

Mirror, Mirror . . .

Consider a full-length mirror your best friend. This is where you're going to get the bare, naked truth—not from your girls and certainly not from the man in your life—who, if he's like most brothers, will try to convince you to "show off" your plump rump and ham-hock thighs. God bless our brothers; we certainly need their affirmation. But remember Mama's words. We're talking professional style here. So . . . back to the mirror. Clad in nothing but your underwear and a smile, stand in front of the mirror and examine the beautiful temple God gave you.

Of course, many of us aspire to the body of a cover model. And because of the images we're fed through the media, some of us probably even think such a body exists. In truth, no one has the perfect body. We all wish that God had doled out a little more of this or a little less of that. What's important here is not how you measure up against the so-called ideal of 36–24–36. What matters is loving and accepting the body you're in. As you look at your fabulous self in that mirror, look a little deeper than the generous hips and thighs, the waistline you wish you had, or the skinny legs you were teased about through grade school. Really look at your body. Note its strength, its power, its grace. Next, go try on a few of your favorite pieces and head back to the mirror. This time don't just stop at "this looks great." Note *why* it looks great. Maybe the sleeveless shift shows off a sexy upper arm. Whatever.

Make a mental note of your body's finer points. Firm bust? Flat stomach? Come now, there's got to be some body part you're proud of. How about a long, elegant neck? Whatever it is, touch it, embrace it, start loving it, and—most important—never, ever wear anything to hide these assets, unless it's too cold. In a nutshell, that's what looking fabulous all the time is all about: putting yourself together in a way that makes the most out of your best. Why do you think certain celebrities always look fabulous? It's not just because they're beautiful and famous (many of them stay on the worst-dressed lists). It's because they pay people, called stylists, whose sole duty is to find the looks that accent their attributes and downplay their flaws. Ever wonder why, despite the fact that she's only around five feet tall, Jada Pinkett Smith always looks long and svelte? Jada always wears body-skimming clothes, so that her petite frame is not enveloped in fabric. What's more, girlfriend knows the power of proportion. She often sports a midriff top to flatter her abs and shows off her legs with daring minis—but almost never will you see her bare both top and bottom at the same time.

Great proportion will rock even an average figure. Below are tips to help you make the best of what *you've* got.

Twenty-five Ways to Look Your Best

1. Find a good tailor. Nothing is more important than proper fit. It can make an expensive outfit look cheap and an inexpensive one look on point.

2. For a slamming, slimming effect, wear one color from head to

toe in a clean, unbroken line. Dark colors, of course, are the best minimizers.

3. When wearing prints, short women look best in small, low-contrast patterns.

4. Taller women—not wider—can wear larger prints with more contrast.

5. Large women needn't avoid prints altogether, but choose wisely. The darker a print's background, the slimmer the look.

6. If you're long-waisted, opt for a short top with a long skirt or pants.

7. If you're short-waisted, the way to go is long top, short skirt.

8. A simple, well-cut suit is a surefire way for any figure to look hot. The jacket should be fingertip length or mid-hip for most women. Go for lean and tapered, but not tight.

9. No matter the "style," find the skirt length that works for you and stick with it.

10. A brightly colored blouse will bring attention to the face.

11. A boat neck does wonders to help minimize your hips and waist and maximize your shoulders.

12. A slim V neck is flattering on just about anyone.

13. A collared shirt will add a few inches to a short torso and frame the face nicely.

14. Turtlenecks highlight a great chin and jawline, while strapless numbers enhance a graceful neck and beautiful skin.

15. A sleeveless, thinly ribbed turtleneck can help minimize the well-endowed bustline.

16. Remember the thong song? Go there if you dare, just avoid panty lines at all costs.

17. The same goes for bras. No one should notice the seams, the color—nothing. Invest in a seamless style to wear under knits and a flesh-tone bra—beige, copper, or brown—never black (unless you're very dark-skinned) to wear under white and light-colored clothes.

18. Try to carry a medium-sized shoulder bag that tucks neatly under your arm. It's the style least likely to add heft to your figure.

19. If you want to lose five pounds instantly, ditch the shopping-bag-size pocketbook.

20. The more open the vamp, or top, of the shoe, the longer your legs will appear.

21. A heel will make your legs look great and the rest of your body thinner. But not only will anything over three inches in the daytime be hard to walk in, it won't look very professional either.

22. Long, dangling earrings can make you look taller.

23. Chokers work best on those blessed with swanlike necks. The rest of us do better with a short, delicate necklace that rests at the base of the neck.

24. Scarves are among the easiest and least expensive ways to add color and change the look of an outfit.

25. No accessory can match confidence. So stand up straight and act like you know you've got it going on—because you do!

Out of the Closet

It's hard to put yourself together if you can't get a handle on what you have in your closet. This was the problem I faced last year. Thanks to the results of my first-ever fitness regimen, each morning as I stood before the mirror I was beginning to see a slimmer and slimmer me. I owned clothes in every size from twelve to eighteen, and my closet was brimming with things that either no longer fit, were outdated, or looked just plain old raggedy.

Many a weekend I'd start the task of paring my wardrobe, to no avail. Then it hit me: I didn't get *into* this closet nightmare in one weekend, and I'm not going to get myself *out* of it in a single Saturday either—especially not by agonizing over every decision to keep or throw away this or that dress.

So I surrendered. I called Melissa Drayton, one of my former staffers in *Essence's* fashion department, and hired her to do the deed. I gave her complete autonomy. After all, who better than a fashion expert—a dispassionate one at that—to decide what in my closet was worth saving or tossing, having altered or repaired? It was one of the smartest moves I've ever made. Now getting dressed in the mornings is a breeze. Everything in my closet is there for a reason, and it's neatly arranged so I can grab what I need when I need it.

Make Over Your Closet

✦ **FIND YOUR OWN MELISSA.** Enlist a friend or someone whose fashion judgment you trust to help you do the wardrobe work. Pop your favorite jams into the CD player and make a night of it.

✦ **EXAMINE EVERY ITEM IN YOUR CLOSET.** Nothing is sacred; justify the space each item is taking up.

✦ **FOLLOW THE ONE-YEAR RULE.** If you haven't worn it, for whatever reason, in the past year, toss it. This goes for things you paid a lot for, things you'll fit into one day, and things you just know will make a comeback.

✦ **ELIMINATE REPEATS.** Black skirts are great, but how many do you really need? Try them all on. Which look great and which look so-so?

✦ **DECIDE THE FATE OF DAMAGED GOODS.** You've been pushing the dress with the tattered hemline to the back of your closet for months now. Whether a garment simply needs new buttons or requires major alterations, decide which clothes are worth repairing and which ones should be retired.

✦ **GET ORGANIZED.** Once you've gone over each item of clothing, rehang everything on good hangers—no wires—that let clothes keep their shape and turn easily so you can see them. Group items together by type—all skirts together, all pants, etc. Then, within each group, organize them by color.

✦ **GET YOUR ACCESSORIES OFF THE FLOOR.** Buy hooks for items like belts, scarves, and pocketbooks.

Follow these same pare-down tips to organize your shoes, sweaters, even lingerie drawers. It may sound like a lot of work, but once you start conquering clutter, you'll find it hard to stop yourself. Order, you see, connotes control. And as we all know, feeling in control is a very powerful thing.

What to Buy

Now that you can clearly see what you have, it's easier to know what you need. Many of us fill our closets with things without even realizing where the voids are in our wardrobes. As a result we always feel—and sometimes, rightly so—that we don't have a thing to wear.

The basics to any sound, professional wardrobe include the following:

+ Classic suit—In a midweight for year-round wear; remember to keep it simple. You can fill in with accessories later.

+ White, cotton blouse—A must-have, it will look great under your suit or paired with pants or a skirt.

+ Silky blouse—For your dressier occasions; should go well with your basic suit.

+ Simple dress—This should be a garment that you dress up for evening or tone down for a business meeting; sheaths work well.

+ Hose—Make sure you keep them in good repair. Own one or two in opaque and a couple pairs of sheer that match your shoes.

The following signature pieces are the purchases I consider "investment items." Here is where you need to spend the most money, for several reasons: These are the items that will take the most wear and tear, so they must be of the highest quality you can afford. These are also the key items that will define your total look. Cheap shoes and/or a cheap handbag will absolutely ruin your outfit. Conversely, a fine pair of shoes and an elegant hand-bag can make a so-so suit or dress look stunning.

◆ Shoes—You probably own several pairs, but be sure you have one basic pair of classic pumps.

◆ Handbag—For business, make sure it goes with your basic pump; it should be medium-sized and in leather, not nylon or vinyl.

◆ Overcoat—You'll need one good coat, because for most of the cold-weather season that's what the majority of the world will see you in. A calf-length style is probably the most practical. It should be in a basic solid color that will accent most of your shoes and handbags.

Be a Smart Shopper

Bear in mind that when I suggest you purchase high-quality pieces, I'm not necessarily saying you must race off to Saks Fifth Avenue and run up your charge cards in a blind frenzy. You can look good without breaking the bank if you know the seven rules of shopping wisely.

◆ **KNOW WHAT YOU NEED.** Your closet has been pared and you're aiming for a classic look to put you on the road to suc-cess. So where are the holes in your wardrobe? You know what happens when you go to the grocery store on an empty stom-ach, right? You buy up all the cookies, chips, and other junk your cart can hold. Well, think about the kind of damage you can do by walking into a mall "hungry" for a fashion fix but with no idea what it should be. That's the kind of shopping that got your closet in such a mess in the first place. Make a list and be disciplined. If you need a pair of shoes, leave the sweater sale and the cosmetic gift-with-purchase deal alone.

✦ **KNOW YOUR SHOPPING STYLE.** Maybe you need your best girlfriend along for good style advice and an honest second opinion. On the other hand, maybe she's the one who gets you into trouble, convincing you to splurge on leather pants or some such when what you set out for is a good interview suit. When you have serious shopping needs, decide before stepping out whether solo or tag team works best for you. And stick to that strategy. Most department stores also have personal shoppers who can guide you when you're looking for that special something or need to coordinate a certain look.

✦ **GIVE YOURSELF ENOUGH TIME.** Don't wait until the evening before your big presentation to look for a new blouse. When you're pressed for time, you're bound to overspend and end up with something you're not wholly satisfied with. By the same token, if you're out shopping for hours and your feet start hurting or you get a headache, go home. Don't feel you have to get something today just because. When you don't feel well, you can't make good purchasing decisions.

✦ **MAKE A BUDGET.** And stick to it. If you're one of those sisters who gets to the checkout counter and starts whispering prayers to the credit-card gods because you're at or near your charge limit, this rule is especially for you. Decide before you leave the house how much you can spend. Be realistic. Of course, we'd all like to look down at the price tag and see the word "FREE" in big, bold letters. But that's not going to happen. You should also establish a list of priorities. If you want to get a new dress, a handbag, and a few scarves, get the big things first. Don't buy three designer scarves only to realize later that you can't afford the dress you want.

+ **VISIT HIGH-END DESIGNER SHOPS.** Even if you can't afford them. This may sound crazy to some people, but hear me out. People who dress well are not necessarily the people who spend the most on clothes. They're the folks who know how to spend. If you're too intimidated to walk in and try on exclusive designer brands, you'll never know what superior quality looks or feels like. Visiting expensive stores will give you the style education you need to make informed purchasing decisions. Many people go to outlet stores today, thinking everything on the racks is a good value. That's not the case. I'm all for outlet shopping, but some of what they offer is junk with a fancy label sewn inside. Specialty boutiques help you understand and distinguish designer brands. Besides, even exclusive boutiques have sales.

+ **DRESS THE PART.** If you've ever seen me out on weekends clad in sweats and a T-shirt, you're probably thinking, "She's a fine one to talk." But trust me, when it comes to serious shopping for key items, I don't mess around. You can't really get a feel for whether or not a dress works when you're wearing big, raggedy underpants, your shoddiest bra, and knee socks. I'm not going to tell you to set out on Saturday dressed like you're going to a Monday-morning meeting, but at least carry some of the things (like maybe shoes and hose) you know you need to make a good purchase decision.

+ **LOVE IT OR LEAVE IT.** Remember how long it took to clear all that mess out of your closet? Don't start junking it up again just because you think, "It looks all right, but I can always use a red blouse" or because an item is on clearance for only

$19.99. A $20 sale item is $20 too much for something you're not going to get a lot of wear out of. When you get dressed in the morning, you want to feel like you're jamming, not just okay. Buy things that move you, things you know will make you feel good to put on your body each day.

Chapter 8

LOVING FAMILY AND FRIENDS

$\mathcal{M}$any who look at a bootstrapper's humble roots—things such as our modest backgrounds, ordinary education, and working-class parents—have a tendency to jump to the wrong conclusion. "That person is a self-made success," they often say.

Nonsense. There's no such thing.

Make no mistake, a bootstrapper does indeed excel largely by dint of her character and determination. She is strong-willed, independent, and driven to hard work and accomplishment. But self-made? No way.

No one in this world makes it alone, especially not a boot-strapper. We have come this far on the backs of many who have gone before us. And because we are natural consensus builders, we boast a universe of teammates, soul mates, and family members. It is their love, faith, and support—and sometimes the lack of it—that make us strong, driven, and creative. Family and friends enrich our lives and help shape us into the women we are. They empathize with our struggles, encouraging us to pick ourselves up and try again. They rejoice in our celebrations, and they share our pain.

I know I would be nowhere without the unfailing support of my husband, Glenn, the good-natured spirit of my daughter, Glynn, my parents' undeniable faith in me; and my girlfriends Jackie, Crystal, Rosemarie, Michelle, and Benilde—who always listen without judgment.

Not only does a strong circle of loved ones *feel* good to you, but tight-knit bonds are also good *for* you. Many medical experts in the field of mind-body research have concluded that stress increases the likelihood of all kinds of disease. And one of the best ways to mitigate the effects of stress is through close relationships. In fact, the medical experts have found that a network of close friends can actually extend your life expectancy.

More than anyone, we sisters need support. And most of us value and honor our sister circles. If you are that Strong Black Woman—struggling to balance your many roles in life—don't make the mistake of thinking you don't need someone to lean on sometime. We all need to lighten the loads of our pressure-filled lives with a trusted confidante—someone for whom we play no role, someone with whom we can just "be."

That is the comfort of my circle of friends and family. When I'm with them, I'm simply me, a down sister from northwest D.C., who likes to laugh, kick back, and have a good time. The many people in my life are truly a blessing. Their closeness is the result of a lifetime commitment of giving and sharing and loving. And our roots run deep.

The Friendship Filter

Some people say that you don't choose your friends, your friends choose you. I think that saying is only half right. Sure, when you're young, many of your partners come by way of shared experiences—maybe you both grew up around the way or went to school together. But I think as you mature, it's important to become discerning where your relationships are concerned. Simply put, your friendships should inspire you, nurture you, embolden you, and generally help you become a better you.

I have been blessed, but I've also been choosy. I'm a very loyal person, and I've always sought out relationships with people who share and honor my ideals of honesty and trustworthiness.

From a very early age I was taught that not everyone who smiles in your face has got your back. I learned to be very selective about whom I let into my inner circle. Even as far back as high school I knew the difference between those folks who wanted to hang in order to mooch a ride—I had use of an old clunker, but, hey, it had four wheels!—and those who stood alongside me when I was at the bus stop. And I still have that keen instinct.

In my business you have to. A journalist wields a certain amount of power. Depending upon the medium, a story that mentions a person's new line of products, for example, can help catapult that person from obscurity to stardom. When I was editor of *Essence*, I was even more aware that lots of folks were attracted not to me as a person but to what they saw as my glamorous role or potential to help them. As a result, I received lots of flowers, fancy invitations, and calls to my office from people who identified themselves as "friends" to my secretary in the same breath that they pronounce my name "Monica." But I know—and I hope you do, too—that friends are the people who honor your whoness, not your whatness.

Your friendships should reflect you, the person you are right now as well as the person you aspire to be. Maybe you're the sister who has a big crew—women you shop with, club with, and gossip with. But how many of them are really your friends? Are they truly feeling you? Are they in touch with who you are as well as what you are? If the answer is no, trust me, you really don't have much in the way of friendship. What you have are associates or acquaintances. There's nothing wrong with having a few of those. But you'd better recognize that these are not the folks to whom you entrust your innermost thoughts.

Your friends are those people who identify with you on a deep level. What's more, as a bootstrapper you need friends who are also in some way role models for you. Naturally this doesn't mean that because you'd like one day to become chief executive of a big corporation, you can only hang out with big-time CEOs. But it does mean that, for example, you should try to seek out relationships with sisters whose leadership skills you admire. Or maybe sisters whose organizational skills you can emulate.

Some people might think this sounds calculating. But you simply must make sure that the relationships with whomever you choose to spend time with are mutually beneficial. I'm not advocating that you dump all your old running buddies once you identify where you want to go in life. A sister who is well organized and efficient could just as easily be a stay-at-home mom or a professional middle manager. The important thing is that you can help each other grow.

If you can't do that, you'll probably find yourself either holding on to relationships that have little value to you or gradually pulling away from certain folk. How many of us can list right now a few sisters with whom we chat often—maybe even meet for lunch or drinks occasionally—and have absolutely nothing in common with anymore? Sure, there may be the superficial things, like mutual associates or events to catch up on. But perhaps they're not as goal-oriented as you are. You don't relate to one another on an emotional level or spiritual tip.

Right here, right now, give yourself permission to let go of such folk. It is perfectly okay to distance yourself from those who are not going your way. Not to unceremoniously kick them to the curb, but to *separate* yourself—at least mentally—from the people you don't want to be like. Maybe, back in the day you enjoyed a close circle of sister-friends you made the club circuit with, a group you shared fashion and beauty secrets with, and so on. Nothing wrong with that. But what happens when, years later, you've tired of the party-girl lifestyle? When instead of hanging out till dawn, you want to turn in early and put in a good, productive day's work? Maybe you're ready to skip happy hour on Friday, so you can be refreshed for the computer courses you've enrolled in at your local community college.

It can be very painful once you realize that you've outgrown a long friendship. But it's absolutely essential that you surround yourself with a circle who will love you and encourage you as you try to change your life for the better. It's not as if you have to stop associating with these sisters altogether. But you certainly cannot give them the time and attention you did when you shared similar interests.

Don't guilt out over it. After all, solid relationships don't end, really; they just change.

A Dream Team

Many of us know in our hearts that some of the friendships we have no longer serve us well, but we're reluctant to let go. Look at your own circle of sisters and try to objectively judge the quality of these relationships. As you start to develop a true sense of personal success, you'll come to the point where you don't tolerate the relationships that no longer charge you. Instead, you'll develop keen antennae for those kinds of people who *add* to the quality of your life. In short, you'll come to build a dream team—a loyal complement of folks who have got your back through this journey called life, a group to whom you can give as much as receive.

Your dream team should be made up of those with whom you share your strongest bond. More than merely fun to be around, they're the people you connect with on the deepest of levels, including:

✦ Spirituality

✦ Intellectual interests

✦ Sense of community or humanity

✦ Career objectives

✦ Emotional disposition

If, by choice or circumstance, you don't have a support network, you can certainly create one. You should aim to have a circle of folks who complement who you are, rather than mirror your every emotional and spiritual experience. And remember the role you play in each other's lives: You want to critique more than criticize; nurture, not negate.

You might need to look no further than your own family or existing crop of friends for deeper, more supportive relationships. For example, maybe you and your best friend talk on the phone almost daily, yet you seldom spend an evening devoted exclusively to baring your souls. Make a commitment to each other now to fortify your bond with regular, meaningful encounters.

If you're virtually starting from scratch, don't dismay. You can still build an effective circle of supporters. All of us know of a person or two we work with or run into occasionally with whom we seem to have a lot in common. These are often folks we would like to get to know but simply haven't taken the opportunity to do so. Perhaps instead of saying to each other for the zillionth time, "We should get together sometime," take out your daily planner and set a date for dinner.

If you are new to a city or otherwise feeling disconnected from a sister-circle, you can also make it your business to meet or attract certain people to your dream team by putting yourself out there and getting involved in activities or causes you care about. It may sound weird, but one of the first places you can check out is the newspaper. While most major dailies carry personal ads for romantic hookups, many also list personal ads for people who are just seeking friendships.

You might also try a few other ways to meet people, including:

+ **SPECIAL INTEREST GROUPS.** Theater groups, political caucuses, and book clubs are specifically designed to bring like-minded folks together. Try to make sure the organization you join includes plenty of opportunity for socializing and discussion in addition to the pursuit of its special interest, so you're sure to have a chance to connect with others.

+ **CONTINUING-EDUCATION CLASSES.** Just for fun, enroll in a class or workshop at your local adult-education center. Photography lessons, wine tastings, and other group-centered classes hold optimum chances of interaction.

+ **COMMUNITY GROUPS.** If you feel especially vested in your community and what happens to it, this is the perfect way to meet others who are civic-minded. You can join your local neighborhood association and meet people at the same time that you exercise a voice in the future of your community.

Remember, no sister is an island. We all need each other. Bootstrappers—for whom life is filled with people but sometimes lonely just the same—need to find balance and peace within a solid group of trusted souls.

Agitator Versus Motivator

Relationships require work—and lots of it. So before you invest your time and energy, make sure your relationships work for you.

I'm especially deft at distinguishing friends from foes—which is not always as obvious as you might think. There are, for example, lots of women who genuinely position themselves as friends yet never miss a chance to chip away at a sister's self-esteem with sly insults or cheap, backstabbing maneuvers. I call them "faux friends." Like carbon monoxide, these folks are toxic. Because their negativity is masked behind kindly gestures and the guise of friendship, it is sometimes easy to get sucked in by them.

Maybe they're jealous or resentful of your drive and determination. So rather than rejoice when you reach a milestone, certain so-called friends might find a way to discount it. For example, you get a much-longed-for promotion, and instead of offering her congratulations, one of these faux friends might say something like "Oh, that's nice, I guess. But you'll be miserable once you start putting in all those hours." Or let's say you've just lost five pounds a couple of weeks after beginning your new exercise program. Rather than tell you how good you look, she says, "Your butt doesn't look quite so huge in those pants you're wearing today."

Likewise, you have to beware of the kind of friends who drain you—the ones who may mean well but drive you to distraction with their constant whining negativity. Mired in a messy swamp of misery, these folks will zap your energy when what they really need is professional help. Many of us sisters, always striving to do the "right" thing, were brought up to believe that we should try to help such souls. That somehow, if they have us to talk to, they might find their way or get better. Don't believe the hype. It may work that way in the movies, but the reality is that you—all by your lonely—cannot save other people from themselves.

Examine your current relationships closely and root out those individuals who—intentionally or not—ultimately bring you down. As you seek to form or widen your support circle, keep an eye out for these types of personalities. They will serve to agitate you more than motivate you.

+ **VICKIE VICTIM.** This is the person who can never seem to get ahead because she is convinced that some external force is working against her. Rather than hold herself accountable, she thinks her parents, her man, the whole world is somehow conspiring to make life miserable for her. She is the undisputed champion of the blame game.

+ **KEISHA QUEEN.** Like the movie star who blabs on and on about herself, then says to her supposed best friend, "Enough about me; what about you—what do *you* think about me?", this sister is the star of the show, and you are relegated to the position of adoring fan. The events in your life barely measure a blip on the radar screen, while her every sneeze warrants a major press conference. Someone so self-absorbed needs a totally one-sided relationship. She has no room for friends, only fans.

✦ **BITTER BONIFA.** Nothing is worse for her than seeing you or someone else succeed. She's happiest when she's belittling someone else and finds a way to rain on your every good fortune. Usually this attitude is a flimsy shield put up to conceal hurt feelings and low self-esteem.

✦ **ALWAYS-RIGHT RHONDA.** In this corner . . . You say up, she says down. You say right, she says left. Let's call the whole thing off. This sister has to be right at all costs, and she will argue you down to the bitter end to prove a point. A conversation with her is exhausting, not only because of the dueling, but because she is ultimately a very poor listener who hears what you have to say only long enough to formulate a comeback.

✦ **NEEDY NITA.** Talk about a bugaboo! She leaves voice-mail messages, e-mails, and blows up your pager. Nita can't stand to be alone, and she's in need of constant praise and attention—this girl is all over you like a cheap slip. She wants to do everything together and cannot bear to make a decision by herself. You may sympathize with her, but what she needs is a nursemaid, not a friend.

When you have these kinds of "friends" in your circle, it's high time to make some important decisions. The healthiest thing for you to do is limit your exposure to such characters, either by eliminating them from your life altogether or by simply reducing the amount of time you elect to share with them. In the same way that good vibes are infectious, so, too, are negative vibes—which is why surrounding yourself with agitators is tantamount to spiritual suicide. Even if you have not identified with any of the agitators listed above, it doesn't mean none exist in your life. Consider the way you feel when you're around certain people.

Generally, agitators bring on certain kinds of feelings, such as anxiety, melancholy, and depression. Ask an agitator-type sister how she's doing, and be prepared for a woe-is-me tale of misery: "Oh, girl, I'm barely hanging on" or "You got a box of Kleenex?" Immediately what you get is a negative pull in the pit of your stomach. Of course, these kinds of folks don't *cause* such feelings. Ultimately, you control how you respond to others. But agitators' personalities help create a climate of doom and make it more difficult to remain focused on a positive path. The most counterproductive thing you can do is to, in effect, play yourself by relying on these kinds of personalities to give you the kind of loyal friendship you want. They're incapable of supplying it, and it's not likely they will change for the better. To varying degrees, each is stuck in her own prison of negativity, from which it will take intense inner work to escape.

To the greatest extent possible, you want to try to surround yourself with motivator types of personalities. These are people who are centered in a positive vibe. They expect the best out of life, and they're determined to get it. You can easily tell when you're around this type of strong personality. When you greet her and ask how she's doing, she's got a positive, upbeat response. Instead of belaboring what's wrong in her life, she focuses on what's going right. She lives with an attitude of gratitude and passes it on to all those she meets. In short, this is a sister who just oozes confidence and warmth.

As you get to know the motivator-type sister on a deeper level, you see in her all the empowering kinds of feelings she represents. For example:

✦ **HONEST ANITA.** Integrity is her trademark. She lives by a strong code of honor and will tell you the truth—tactfully— even when you don't want to hear it.

- ✦ **LISA THE LISTENER.** With both her head and her heart, she receives what you're trying to say. Listening is something she does fully and actively. So when you're talking to her, she's really hearing you and ready to offer constructive criticism and suggestions.

- ✦ **RESPONSIBLE RASHEEDA.** Accountable for her actions and reactions, this is not the type of sister who is sitting around blaming others for her station in life.

- ✦ **PROACTIVE PATTI.** Girlfriend gets it done. In every way, she is serious about her own personal growth and committed to changing her life for the better.

Honoring Your Sister-Circle

I've heard some sisters make the claim that they prefer male friends to females. Citing things like jealousy and backstabbing, they say that men are simply easier to relate to. I feel for the sister who doesn't have a good girlfriend. And frankly, I've always suspected that the reason they find it hard to form friendships with other women is that they are themselves inclined to petty jealousies and disloyal behavior.

There is perhaps no greater bond a woman can share than the close and intimate relationship she experiences with her circle of sister-friends. It is a sacred trust. Many of us reveal things to our girls that we would never in a million years tell a lover or even our mothers—always with the unspoken understanding that our confidence will not be betrayed. Talk about sex, lies, and videotape! Those in our sister-circle probably know us better than anyone on earth. And it is in that all-knowing intimacy that we feel protected, respected, and loved.

What is it that glues us to one another so tightly? And how is it that these kinds of friendships seem to endure longer and stronger than any other—through boyfriend after boyfriend, job after job, and drama after drama? Dating back to preslavery days, we sisters were bound together by our shared tribal experiences. As the providers of the family, our men went off regularly to hunt the food needed to nourish us and the rest of the clan. In their absences we banded together and took care of one another's children.

Back in the day, it was truly a village that raised a child. We remained close on the plantation and throughout Jim Crow and urban migration. But in recent generations something happened. Much like society at large, we became a more individualistic people and lost some of the sense of community that for so many generations held us together. On many levels we have become fissured, divided by status, class, and geography. How can we make the sister-circle strong once again? Stop frontin'. We put up many of the same defenses around "our girls" as we do for the outside world. In other words, our near-maniacal drive to be the Strong Black Woman holding it down precludes us from being completely and totally honest with one another. When is the last time, for example, you broke down and cried with your best friend or revealed your deepest insecurities? In order to achieve real peace, we sisters have to find a way to deal with all of our issues. We truly need one another, but we're so conditioned to be "perfect" that we have a hard time being vulnerable; that means we're less than honest with ourselves and with each other.

To open up the channels of honest communication, success coach and author Erline Belton recommends the following exercise to those she coaches. And she says it is also appropriate for sisters who are committed to growth.

Take a Poll

Get some constructive feedback from people who know you best. Approach some of your closest friends and tell them, "I'm trying to learn about myself; will you help me?" Ask them how they perceive you. Sometimes we have certain intentions and simply assume our actions bear them out. But how are you *really* coming off?

Sort It Out

So there are certain areas your friends seem to agree that you need to work on. But there are also undoubtedly others in which you excel. Say to yourself, "Okay, this is where I'm weak. But this is where I'm jamming."

Max It Out

Make a plan to optimize your strengths to go after the things in life you desire. Again, a strong sister can help you here. But much of your planning will come as a result of intense inner work, such as journaling, visualization, and affirmation.

Our sister-friends are cherished relationships. That's why when a sister-circle breaks or even warps, the emotional fallout can be traumatic. I can remember such a time. It was nearly twenty years ago, but I remember it like it was yesterday. Jackie and Kim, two of my oldest and dearest friends—we go back to tenth grade—confronted me one afternoon shortly after we'd all moved to New York City. They were still finishing their studies, so money was tight and they were experiencing little of the New York life we'd all dreamed of. Meanwhile, I was working—although for a meager salary—and because of the many perks that go along with working in fashion, I was mixing with the "beautiful people" and attending all kinds of fabulous parties. I was busy with my new job at Fairchild, *and* I had a boyfriend.

Together, Jackie and Kim confronted me. They said that I no longer had time for them and that I thought I was better than they were. I was crushed. Here were two of the friendships I cherished most in the world—my girls who I thought knew me better than that. I was hurt and angry. I countered, "No, *you* think I'm better. I refuse to stand here and defend myself." Then I walked out.

The next day I received a very teary phone call from Jackie, offering an apology. She admitted that lately she hadn't been feeling very good about herself. And she told me that when I walked out, she experienced the kind of emptiness she felt when her mother died. I was touched by her honesty. And we were able to pick up our friendship where we left off. I no longer remember how Kim and I came back together, but today I'm closer to both Jackie and Kim than ever before.

In order to have a strong sister-bond, make sure that you are a strong and stable link in the chain. Don't take your girls for granted or abandon them when a new job, love, or other interest comes into your life. If you sense there's a problem between you and your sister-friends, be woman enough to address it. Likewise, when things are going well, speak on that, too. When is the last time you told your best friend that you love her? That you appreciate her for her honesty? Her spirit? Her support?

Once you have an established sister-circle, honor those relationships, and rather than ask "What have you done for me lately?" examine some of the things you can do to make the bond stronger. For example, keep in mind the following:

+ **LOVE AND ACCEPT UNCONDITIONALLY.** So she's your girl, right? So by now you know that she's always running late at least fifteen minutes, that she means well but sometimes forgets to follow up. So why cop an attitude every time she follows form? Accept that she may not always do things as you would. Nor do you have to agree on everything. If you offer your love and support unconditionally, you'll be rewarded with hers.

+ **BE TRUSTWORTHY.** Few things are more important than integrity in a sister-to-sister friendship. In the best of such relationships, you're baring your soul. You can't win the honor of a friend if you're not honorable yourself. Trust is earned gradually, not all at once. So by staying true to your word on small things—honoring get-together dates and keeping your word—you're more likely to win her trust on the big stuff.

+ **SMALL GESTURES MEAN A LOT.** Several years ago my dearest friend was going through some serious changes with her man. And it was no secret to her that most of us in her sister-circle disliked him for the cavalier way in which we thought he treated her. I ran across a greeting card with a cat hanging from a tree that said simply "Hang in there, baby." When I sent it to her, she was practically moved to tears. She said that while many of her friends secretly hoped for the break up of their relationship, my gesture showed that she had my support.

+ **LISTEN WITH YOUR HEART.** Often we think we know what someone—especially someone we've known for a significant time—is going to say. So instead of listening openly, we listen only long enough to formulate our response or judgment. Listening is probably the easiest thing you can do for a friend, but is also the most overlooked.

+ **BE LOYAL.** Has one of your friends ever been the brunt of unkind rumors, or has she ever had to make an unpopular decision? It is in situations like these when it is more important than ever that those in her sister-circle have her back. True loyalty not only demands that you stand by her in the face of adversaries; it also means that you remain loyal within the sister-circle. I have three very close friends who mean a lot to me. It's always disconcerting when one sister in particular speaks disapprovingly of one of us to the other two. Inevitably word gets back, and a bit of trust is chipped away.

✦ **RESPECT BOUNDARIES (ESPECIALLY THE BLURRY ONES).** If you and your best friend go way back, you probably know that she is always there for you. But don't abuse that support by calling on her at any and every time of day. If you know that she and her man went out on Friday, is it really necessary that you call first thing Saturday just to talk about *your* date the night before?

Family Ties

When I decided to open a bed-and-breakfast in the middle of Bedford-Stuyvesant, Brooklyn, I faced many naysayers. "Black folks won't support a black-owned business," people said. "White folks won't support a black business," others warned. I heard it all, and I heard it from all sides.

But the last place I expected to hear the echoes of doubting Thomases was within my own loving, supportive family. Yet my dad voiced his concern from jump street: "What makes you think folks will spend money to stay in *this* run-down house in *this* neighborhood?" he said.

Did it mean he didn't love me? That he didn't have faith in me? Of course not. I challenged my father just to wait and see what I would create. Even though he didn't believe in the plan, he believed in me. So he kept his eyes open for antiques that might fit in well at the inn, and he constantly asked with concern—not with suspicion—"How's it going?"

I share this with you because I think it's very important to realize that even within your strongest sphere of supporters, you can never look to others to cosign your dreams. There will be times when you see things that even your closest blood cannot. And it doesn't make your vision any less valid.

In the end what is important to remember is not that everyone close to you thinks your thoughts and dreams your dreams—no one else can do that anyway.

What matters most sometimes is what those closest to us *don't* do. It matters that they don't disrespect, disparage, or discourage us. It may not seem like much to ask, but for some sisters, family members scrutinize with the sharpest eye and criticize with the most biting tongue.

No one wants tense relations among family. Since they're the closest people to us, it's only natural that we come to rely on them—first and foremost—for love and support. Unfortunately, there are some cases where the most toxic or destructive energy comes not from the outside world but from within the ranks of our blood relations.

What is a woman to do if her mother, for example, constantly puts her down or makes harsh judgments against her lifestyle and generally casts a pall over her entire day? Or if her sister's constant competing pits them against each other and spoils their friendship?

Unlike a friend or associate, a relationship with your mother or other family member is not one you can easily extricate yourself from. But you *can* find ways to disarm toxic kinds of behavior so as to mitigate its negative impacts on your psyche.

I know a sister who has done it and done it well. Michelle is the only girl in her family, and she's always felt a certain responsibility for her now elderly mother. Once Michelle graduated from college, she settled a mere thirty minutes away from her widowed mother and the house in which she grew up. She always made it a point to pay her mother twice-weekly visits, invite her shopping, and attend Sunday services with her. All this despite the fact that she rarely received a word of thanks—or *any* kind words, for that matter. Her mother disliked Michelle's taste in clothes and men and put her down often—once even telling her that "only pretty girls can leave the house with no makeup." Michelle tried talking to her mom about it but got nowhere. Her mother told her she was only trying to help her by telling her things no one else would.

Finally, as she came upon her thirty-fifth birthday, Michelle began making some changes. She got a new man in her life but rarely brought him around her mother or spoke of him. And she cut down drastically on the amount of mother-daughter time they spent together—reducing most weeks to Sunday service and brunch. When her mother's talk turns critical, rather than debate her, Michelle simply tunes her mom out. With no reaction from Michelle, her mother has curbed her criticisms.

And now that Michelle has limited exposure to her, she's actually able to enjoy her mother's company. With another sister I know, the issues lie with her dad. They're very close, but he's also close to Johnnie Walker Red on the weekends. When he's drinking, he's belligerent and says hurtful things to his daughter that he later has no memory of or becomes defensive about. If she senses that her father has been drinking, she reminds him that she will not talk to him while he is under the influence and then politely hangs up the phone. Setting these rules—barriers to pain—is not only helpful, it's healthful.

Draining Relations

We bootstrappers tend to be very family-oriented folk. We honor our family members and support them in any way we can—whether it is physical, emotional, or financial support that they might need. But what's often very difficult to accept is that sometimes there is little we can do to help our relations move forward. At some point we have to let them live their lives not as we would have them live, but as *they* see fit to live.

I know a sister whose entire family struggled to understand and assist Junior—the youngest of four siblings—in his efforts to gain control over his life. Junior is basically a good kid, but since dropping out of high school a year short of graduating six years ago, he drifted from job to job trying to find himself. Still living at home, he "borrowed" money from anyone in the family who would lend it and never repaid his debts. The family wanted him to enter a four-year college and earn a degree. And at various times he seemed to want that, too.

But usually he appeared more concerned with outfitting himself in the latest Air Jordans and trading up on beepers, cell phones, and other techno gadgets. He offered countless excuses as to why he hadn't taken the high school equivalency exam. And the college brochures my girlfriend sent to the house sat in his room unopened and gathering dust.

To everyone on the outside looking in, it was obvious that Junior was not going to change the course of his life until he was ready. Still, my girlfriend continued her rescue mission to "help" her baby brother until he had tapped most of her energy and much of her bank account. A couple of years ago she began saying no to his "loan" requests, and her mom put him out after he ran up a whopping phone bill. Then, several months ago, something interesting happened. After quietly taking and passing the GED test, Junior registered for classes at the local community college.

Many of us have perhaps been in the same position with a family member or someone who is like family to us. We twist ourselves into a pretzel trying to live their lives for them—nearly always to no avail. Then, when we decide to let go, they manage to find their way.

Sometimes the term "letting go" seems to imply giving up. But that's far from the real meaning. To let go is simply to release your expectations and your need to control a situation—release them to God. It is an admission that in all things it is God's will, not our will, that will be done. But it takes a great measure of emotional maturity to do this. Consuming oneself with the problems of others can be, after all, a very convenient distraction. It temporarily relieves us of the responsibility to do our own inner work and allows us to sweat over things that, deep down, we know we have no control of.

But to some extent we've been socialized to believe that worrying and loving are congruent terms, that one naturally accompanies the other. On the contrary, love—when it is deep and unconditional—is wholly accepting of free will. When someone you care about is involved in destructive behavior—whether it is merely mooching, like Junior, or something far more serious, such as drug or alcohol addiction—it is perfectly acceptable to love at a distance. In fact, it's advisable. Note that this is not abandonment, because you don't love the person any less, you just learn to love him or her differently. You suppress the need to intertwine yourself into someone else's dilemma and micromanage someone else's life. Instead, you make assurances that while you love the person, you don't condone the current behavior. Meanwhile, you step back and you pray that the healing will come in time.

Family Funk-tions

There are those rare cases when it is not a single family member who tests our strength but rather the entire clan. Some sisters—bootstrappers in the purest definition of the word—have been forced to rise above a seemingly inbred cycle of negativity and unhealthy behavior within their own families in order to find their truth. I'm talking about the sister who has suffered through a childhood filled with abuse—physical, sexual, verbal—and other injustices. The sister who has grown up in a home dominated by alcohol or drugs. And even the sister who has endured life in an angry, dispirited, or emotionally distant family.

These are the kinds of family units that put the "funk" in dysfunction. Most often they breed discontent—at best. At worst, a dysfunctional childhood can produce adults who suffer from severe depression, anxiety, poor self-esteem, stress-related health problems, and any number of self-destructive lifestyles. Such is the result of growing up without the benefit of a protective sense of love and far too little self-love.

There are all sorts of abuse a person can suffer. And let's face it, what modern experts label child abuse was simply regular old discipline back in the day. Most of our parents grew up with the edict "Spare the rod, spoil the child." Only you can be the judge of whether there was genuine mistreatment. Studies show that many children of dysfunctional upbringings don't even recognize their suffering and assume that their pain is "normal." But if you feel somehow ill at ease around your people, that's a clue that there may be some scars there. Here are a few other tip-offs:

+ You have the feeling that nothing you do will please your people or make them proud of you.

✦ You dread talking to or visiting one or both of your parents and do so out of obligation rather than free will.

✦ You feel as though your parents and your siblings don't really know you, so you don't relate to one another well.

It's no easy task, but you should try to get to the bottom of these feelings. How long have you been experiencing them, and where do you think they might be coming from? You might begin by asking yourself if you felt that your parents demonstrated any of the following types of behavior and whether that behavior left you feeling emotionally crippled or harmed as a result.

Was one or both of your parents:

✦ Overprotective to the point of suffocation?

✦ So driven to perfection that you could never measure up?

✦ Unduly harsh in their punishments?

✦ Cold or unemotional to the point where you didn't hear the words "I love you"?

✦ Manipulative—pulling emotional strings or pushing certain buttons to keep you under control?

✦ Absent, both emotionally and physically?

✦ Victims of some major childhood trauma themselves; i.e., sexual or substance abuse, mental illness?

✦ Either estranged from or locked into bitter battles with their own parents?

If any of these issues recall your upbringing, you may consider therapy to help work through the difficulties of your past, because when the dysfunctions of our childhood don't just magically disappear once we become adults, those issues that are left unresolved often end up being repeated. And those unhealthy patterns continually dog us and keep us from the success we desire.

As I've said before, no one ever claimed that life was fair. And while it's unfortunate that we're not all blessed with loving, well-adjusted, and supportive families, there *is* still hope. With some help and a lot of hard work—trust me, sister—you *can* learn to make peace with your past and take your rightful place in the world.

Perhaps you know of a remarkable sister who has managed to fight through the emotional prison in which she was raised to go on to lead a rewarding life. I do, and she is an inspiration to me and everyone who meets her.

Chandra was born in East St. Louis, Illinois, the fourth child born to a nineteen-year-old mother who never married any of her babies' daddies. Chandra's father was gone before she was even born. To say that Chandra grew up poor would be an understatement, and it was the least damaging of the ills she suffered. She and her brothers and sisters were often left alone to fend for themselves, and Chandra says she can't recall ever hearing "I love you." Her young mother had little self-respect and gained quite a reputation within the small community for her sexual exploits with a variety of men. The one good aspect of this was that when a man was in the picture, the children were relatively well taken care of—at least physically.

Theirs was a household where hope and optimism were in short supply. Chandra's mother believed that life had handed her a raw deal and that her children were destined to the same fate. None of the children was encouraged to attend school. And while her siblings ran the streets, Chandra looked forward to her classes, saying it was the only place she felt a sense of structure and support. She read voraciously, and with the help of a guidance counselor she received a scholarship to Loyola University in Chicago after graduating high school with honors.

Today Chandra, who admits to being angry with her mother for years, is not the least embittered, despite the pain she endured as a little girl. And she credits her emotional health to "a combination of constant prayer and off-and-on therapy." Although they live dramatically different lifestyles, she communicates with her mother and three siblings—all of whom still live in East St. Louis with their mother and jump sporadically between public assistance and menial jobs. They seem to regard Chandra as the "rich" one, and frequently she is called upon for loans. Since she has come to learn that the so-called loans are never repaid, she obliges only occasionally. Chandra says that if not for her mother's less-than-nurturing parenting style, she might never have spent so much time alone examining her thoughts and "discovering myself."

"My mother did the best she could with what she had," she adds. "It wasn't much, but my only choice was to move my own life forward or let her psyche trap me."

Psychology experts say that Chandra accomplished what many sisters in similar situations rarely manage to pull off. Growing beyond childhood dysfunction demands three things if a person has any hope of overcoming years of anger and hurt.

1. **Leave the nest.** In other words, put some emotional distance between you and your family. Declare your independence.

2. **Balance it out.** Nurture other relationships so that your family is not your only resource of love and support.

3. **Redefine your life.** There is far more to you than being so-and-so's daughter. Set your ideals and values simply even if they aren't the ones you grew up with.

Find One Hundred Ways

How do you want to be remembered by those you love most? Would you want them to recall your great job title? How much money you made? How well you dressed? Of course not. Most of us want our loved ones above all to know how much they mean to us.

Yet at the end of the day how many of us can say we went out of our way to let them know it? I'll be the first to admit it: I can get so caught up in the day-to-day craziness of life that I neglect to tell the one person closest to me—my husband, Glenn—that I love and appreciate him. Now, it's nothing for him to turn around out of the blue and say something like "You're the best. I love you." Of course, I love to hear that. Who wouldn't? We all thrive on those sweet nothings. I'm reminding myself right now to let him know how much he means to me more frequently—through word and deed.

My parents and siblings are, unfortunately, two hundred miles away in my hometown of Washington, D.C. Every Sunday I call home and "check in." But there have been times when I have forgotten a birthday, made the "Happy Father's Day" call on the following Monday, or sent the shower gift long after the joyous occasion. And I have dear friends, like Karen in Atlanta, whom I've known since elementary school, who reaches out and touches far more often than I do, but she never makes me feel guilty about it. I'm so grateful for her.

I have simply asked Karen and all of my loved ones to be patient with me, as I continue to become more skilled at balancing my many roles and responsibilities. When we do talk on the phone or get together, I make sure I let them know how much I love them and appreciate their support, compassion, and patience. My husband and I even held a lavish "appreciation" dinner one year to say thank you for the love and the friendship, and happy birthday, happy anniversary, congratulations and any other such heartfelt expression we neglected to wish in a timely manner. We're now planning to take our families on a cruise, because we're lusting for some quality time with them.

I've come to discover that I'm not alone in wanting to spend more time with the people who matter most to me. A few years ago, the NBC newsmagazine *Dateline* polled five hundred people and asked how they would choose to spend an extra hour of time—if they were lucky enough to get one, that is. More than 75 percent said they would elect to spend more time with their loved ones. All of us live hectic lives, in one way or another. We have daily obligations to our professions, our families, or both. And because our schedules are so jam-packed, we have less and less time to connect with one another on anything but a superficial level. Add to that the fact that technology now allows us to communicate by cell phone, e-mail, and fax, and it's easy to see why most of us find old-fashioned person-to-person interaction so difficult to come by—and so precious when we do.

One of the things I've discovered about the people closest to us is this: They simply need to know what they mean to us from time to time. That means letting go of a lot of the so-called obligatory holidays and occasions and getting close to your peeps on the regular. After all, it can sometimes be difficult to remember a birthday or anniversary; however, it is not hard to think about how much you love those key people in your life. Despite your busy schedule, you can reach out and touch someone you care about. Here are a few ways to do it almost effortlessly:

✦ In the middle of the day, even when you know the person may not be at home, call and leave an "I love you" message on the machine. Or for the computer-savvy, e-mail a note.

✦ Send flowers or candy for no apparent reason.

✦ Buy a box of postcards or blank cards and keep them in your office. Jot a "love" note to your mom, your sibling, or your man, expressing your feelings. If you travel often, put some in your travel bag.

✦ When you get a new daily planner or electronic organizer, input significant dates immediately. Do the same with your desk calendar at work.

✦ Designate a day or time for touch-base calls. For me, it's Sunday evening, when I religiously call my parents.

✦ Drop a note of recognition, even if you remember a special date late. Even belated greetings express warm wishes and show you care.

✦ If you have children, send off their class pictures as soon as you get them back.

✦ Children also come in handy when you don't have time to get a fancy store-bought card; give the little ones some paper and let the creativity flow.

✦ Share tough decisions. Even if you already know how you'll resolve an issue, touch base to get your loved ones' input. It will make them feel needed and included in your life.

✦ Extend invitations to your friends—even for little things. If you and a close friend work near one another, arrange to meet for a manicure in the afternoon. Or plan to grocery shop together.

✦ Use the Internet to send loved ones small tokens, such as a book or CD you think they might enjoy.

+ Establish date nights on a monthly or bimonthly basis with friends, family, and lovers—setting aside time for a special get-together.

+ End every conversation with "I love you."

Chapter 9

LEAVING THE WORLD A BETTER PLACE

$\mathcal{M}$ost of us look at the world or look around our communities and are made keenly aware of the need for change. We can't help but see the crime, economic deprivation, inferior schools, social ills, health challenges, homelessness, hopelessness. Sometimes the need is so great that we get overwhelmed and retreat, seeing ourselves as powerless little cogs in a much larger machine, with little or no ability to make a difference. I understand.

Oftentimes in the space of an hour I'm forced to acknowledge many hard realities. I wake up and turn on the morning news and see another one of our men handcuffed and headed off for a penal institution that has become little more than a racket. I get dressed and head for the subway, dodging somebody else's dog's doo in my path. A mountain of household rubbish and other debris stands tall on the corner of one block, as if it were some kind of shrine, meant to be there. Meanwhile, my brothers stand small on the opposite corner, reminding me that far too few of our men are gainfully employed. The lady walking in front of me pulls her bag a little closer as she passes by them, a brutal confirmation that crime and danger do exist and that there is victimization born out of desperation.

Once I board the train, I see our children eating their substandard breakfast—potato chips—and getting off at the stop for the substandard school, where 90 percent of the students read below grade level. And the toddler sitting across from me? She won't sit still, so she gets cursed publicly by a mother who's privately living in hell. A few seats down sits a well-dressed businessman; next to him, a ragged-looking homeless sister who just plopped down after walking the car with her hand out, begging for money for food.

It's only 9:00 A.M., yet I feel like I want to turn around, go back home, and get into bed.

Instead, I remind myself of the examples set by Rosa Parks, Ida B. Wells, Fannie Lou Hamer, Mary McCloud Bethune. I've already accepted that I alone can't change the world, but maybe I can say some kind words to that mother with the fidgety child. Maybe I can acknowledge her challenges and praise her youngster so that she might feel good enough about herself to see the good in her child, if only in that moment.

If you're committed enough, you may see even greater gain. When Glenn and I decided to open our bed-and-breakfast in Bedford-Stuyvesant, our mission was far bigger than simply putting heads on beds. We wanted to provide a place our people could be proud of, a place where they would be treated as the kings and queens they are, a restorative respite where individuals could come and recharge themselves to go back out into the community and do the critical work we must all do. The comments and reflections left by our guests in the room journals is proof that our mission is being actualized— and motivation for us to keep on keepin' on. Consider these entries:

"We came here at odds with one another, desperately needing the time and place to reconnect and reacquaint ourselves with the person we fell in love with. Now we are stronger as individuals, as a couple, and as soldiers for our people."

"I am here with me, myself, and I. I just needed a break. I have been renewed."

"In this place surrounded by African artifacts, I feel the presence of our ancestors and I am at peace."

People from the neighborhood who have never spent the night at the inn have been positively affected, too. Once, as I was giving a fifth-grade class a tour of Akwaaba, a little girl asked, "Is this a mansion?" When I replied yes, she looked somewhat unimpressed and said, "That's nice. But when I grow up, I'm gonna live in a castle!" My response: "You go, girl!"

When the mansion is featured on TV and in newspapers, neighborhood folk become a little prouder of where they live. The acknowledgment of the community's architectural richness becomes great ammunition for the many who often feel they have to defend the place they call home. Now Bedford-Stuyvesant, the second-largest community of black folks anywhere in the country, is in the news constantly. And it's not a gloom-and-doom story. One of the latest headlines was on the cover of *New York* magazine, proclaiming Bedford-

Stuyvesant as one of the six New York City areas where you can still afford to buy your dream home. While we shouldn't depend on others outside of ourselves to validate us, I have noticed a difference in the way we feel about and treat our neighborhood since we started getting all the press. For so long, because of broken glass and litter on our streets, we failed to recognize that we were still walking on diamonds and pearls. Our properties have real value. More important, our people do. Real estate prices are now soaring, and we're sweeping up in front of our homes and demanding that the Department of Sanitation do its part, too.

One of our disappointments when moving to Bed-Stuy a decade ago was the lack of basic amenities other neighborhoods took for granted. I wanted a nearby place where I could have coffee with a friend, too. I wanted a spot where I could pick up fresh flowers on my way home from the subway. An ice cream parlor where my daughter and I could have a treat would be nice. And how about a bookstore? A fine restaurant?

We decided to not let this lack keep us away, but instead to see it as an opportunity to help build a community. It's been five years since we opened Akwaaba Mansion and two years since the opening of Akwaaba Café, our elegant restaurant down the street, which features live jazz and poetry on specific nights. Only a few months have passed since we opened Mirrors, our new coffeehouse, in a commercial building we purchased next door to the restaurant. Mirrors debuted in the building along with Brownstone Books and The Parlor Floor Antiques, businesses owned by husband-and-wife team Crystal and Walston Bobb-Semple, who also live in the neighborhood. What gives me real joy is knowing that we can now circulate our dollars in our own neighborhood and employ our own. The community has been incredibly supportive, and not once has anyone even written graffiti on the front of the businesses—a big deal in New York!

I am somewhat relentless in my dedication to the community. I serve on several boards, including the Bridge Street Development Corporation, which is doing much of the housing and economic development in the area, and on Community Board #3, which is our neighborhood liaison for the borough's government. All proposals and problems—from public-transportation changes to trash-pickup complaints—must pass through the Community Board.

I'm also dedicated to helping improve the school district. My husband and I send our nine-year-old daughter to public school in the area, because as products of public education ourselves, we believe in it. We also don't think our daughter should have to go out of her community, away from her friends there, to get a decent education. So we try to make her school work for us as much as we can. We interview her teacher at the beginning of the school term and stay in constant contact throughout the year. We sit in the class during open-school weeks, stay active with the PTA, and supplement anything we think the curriculum might be lacking with outside activity—like enrolling Glynn in weekend music and computer classes.

For me, choosing to make a difference in the world through my community is a way of life, one I come by honestly. When I was growing up in Washington, D.C., my parents were very active in the neighborhood. Ours was the house where all the kids on the block gathered. Many a weekend my dad could be found piling my three brothers and a gaggle of neighborhood boys into the family station wagon or his pickup truck and heading off to a baseball or football game. As one of the few fathers present in the area, he was also the man who took kids to the empty parking lot to practice their driving skills.

Mom, meanwhile, was just as much a doer. She volunteered as a leader of my Brownie troop. At our church she was the youth leader, planning activities for the teens and helping us to form a young-adult gospel choir. Both my parents have always been members of civic groups that performed community service. And though most of the time our family struggled to make ends meet, on holidays like Christmas and Thanksgiving we always put together baskets of food and gifts for those in our community less fortunate than ourselves.

Yes, You Can Make a Difference

As a people, we have always been altruistic. We have taken to heart the words of our ancestors—mantras like "Each one, teach one" and "It takes a village to raise a child." Most of us really do want to give back. We understand that we as individuals haven't truly made it unless we as a people do. Maybe you've found it difficult to make the time to give back, but it doesn't take much. The world is counting on you. Here are some easy ways to make a difference:

✦ CIVIL RIGHTS ORGANIZATIONS. The National Urban League, the National Association for the Advancement of Colored People, the National Council of Negro Women . . . to name a few. Make it your business to be a dues-paying, card-carrying member of these generations-old groups that have done so much to uplift the race and protect the hard-won rights to which we are entitled. (National Association for Colored People, 1-410-521-4939, www.naacp.org; National Urban League, 1-212-558-5300, www.nul.org; National Council of Negro Women, 1-202-737-0120)

✦ **GOVERNMENT.** You don't have to be an elected official to be involved in the political process. The simplest way to get active in the inner workings of local, state, or federal government is to volunteer to help a candidate or cause you believe in. You might assist in a voter-registration drive, stuff envelopes at a campaign headquarters, or distribute petitions to get an official elected or an issue on the ballot. Once politicians are in office, hold them accountable. Know what their voting record is and challenge them to really act on behalf of you, their constituent.

✦ **SORORITIES AND FRATERNITIES.** Black Greek organizations have been around since the early 1900s, and they have a long record of community activism. Joining one that appeals to you is an easy way to become involved in scholarship drives, health fairs, and other events that benefit your brothers and sisters.

✦ **MENTORING.** When you give a young person the benefit of your time and your experience, you plant seeds of confidence and future success. Big Brothers/Big Sisters conducted a study demonstrating that kids involved in mentoring relationships are less likely to use illegal drugs, skip school, or get into fights. (Big Brothers, Big Sisters of America 1-215-567-7000, www.bbbsa.org)

✦ **CHURCH.** Traditionally, the black community's strength has resided in its churches. You can join or launch any program designed to feed the homeless, help the elderly, tutor the youth, or perform other outreach services.

✦ **BLOCK OR NEIGHBORHOOD CLUB.** Sometimes the best place to begin making a dent is right outside your front door.

Organize your neighbors to form a crime-watch committee or just to keep your area clean and polished. If you feel really inspired, you can even begin to work together to lobby your local politicians to make improvements in the neighborhood.

✦ **BLACK BUSINESSES.** Sister and brother entrepreneurs need our patronage. It is only through building economic wealth that we as a people can truly effect change in American society. Dry cleaners, printers, grocers, restaurants—make it your business to know which businesses in your city or town are black-owned, and give them your loyal support.

✦ **MARCHES.** During the civil rights movement of the 1960s, brothers and sisters were able to focus the entire nation's attention on the injustice of segregation simply by banding together and walking peaceably for the causes in which they believed. We can do the same today. Step up and stand up for the causes that move you.

✦ **CHARITABLE DONATIONS.** If you see a homeless person shivering in the cold, give her your scarf. The next time you read or hear about devastation—whether it's famine in Africa or a fire across town—don't just say, "What a shame." Donate clothes, money, whatever you can spare.

Am I making a difference? You better believe it. But the biggest difference is happening in me. As I seek to empower or inspire somebody else, I get stronger and I become encouraged by my results, no matter how small they may seem. The fact is, even the smallest positive action has the potential to affect others. We can begin to change the world simply by smiling at strangers, by being loyal to our friends, by allowing kindness and compassion to temper our words. I know that if I can make a difference in even one person's life, that's a powerful act. My love and support of another can be like a stone tossed into the lake, rippling out to everyone whose heart that person touches. So tap that power in yourself. Use it consciously. Use it for good. Because in the end, that's what truly matters.

EPILOGUE

Coming Full Circle

At the beginning of this book, I confessed that I, too, am a work in progress. I end this book in the exact same physical space where I started it—on the beautiful beach of Cape May, New Jersey, with my face to the sun and my toes in the sand. Yet I am at an entirely different place in my life. No doubt, I am still a bonafide bootstrapper—one who is willing to work long and hard to achieve success, as I've uniquely defined it for myself. But, I have grown tremendously, and I have the writing of this book to thank for it.

I told you that I was going to ride shotgun with you on this journey to self-actualization. Well, I'm proud to report that I've made a couple of U-turns in my life that are leading me down a new and exciting road. I'm sure that like all roads, this one will have its bumps, but then I'm no longer driving one hundred miles an hour.

You see, as much as I loved my year and a half as editor in chief of *Essence,* I've made the hard decision to free myself of the strong black woman syndrome by leaving it. I knew I could continue to lead the nation's number one magazine for black women, run my three businesses, remain active in my community, and devote myself to being a "present" wife and mother. But I also knew that I, Monique, would continue to be at the end of my very long to do list, especially given the fact that my husband and I were about to launch our fourth business venture, Akwaaba by the Sea, the only black-owned inn in the historic seaside resort town of Cape May, ninety minutes by car from Philadelphia.

In a moment of reflection (following a few hours of some serious number crunching), I realized that my bootstrapping ways over the past twenty years have paid off. I saw that it was now financially possible for me to change my course, and I thanked God for the blessing.

And so, a few weeks before the first guests were scheduled to arrive at the door of Akwaaba by the Sea, I resigned as editor in chief of *Essence*. My time at the magazine had been so much more than just a job to me. It had been an extraordinary mission—a chance to help black people live spiritually rich and fulfilling lives. Now I planned to continue that mission by providing a place where my sisters and brothers could relax and revive their spirits, something I looked forward to doing more of myself. I was nervous (no steady paycheck) and melancholy (I would surely miss the daily company of coworkers who were dear friends), yet thrilled by the possibilities of my reworked life. There's one thing I was not— and that was worried about my identity. Being the editor of *Essence* is what I did, not who I was. Lacking that understanding trips up many a sister fortunate enough to ascend to a job with a fancy title.

Responses to my decision were mixed at first. When I told one friend about my leaving the magazine, she responded only half-jokingly, "Now I won't be able to brag about my girlfriend being the editor in chief of *Essence*." I paused, then said, "I hope you'll be proud to talk about your girlfriend who is editor of her own life, taking out some parts to put emphasis on other parts."

And when I told my nine-year-old daughter, Glynn, that Mommy would no longer be working at *Essence*, she looked alarmed and shouted, "Why?" I was stunned by her reaction and reminded her of how she always said she wanted me to pick her up from school and help her with her homework. I explained that now I would be able to. "But how are we going to pay our bills? How are we going to live in this house and have food on the table," she asked with concern.

Her questions made sense because every time I couldn't accompany her class on a trip, or had to work late for the fourth time in the week, or go away on business, I would explain to her that Mommy has to go to work so we can afford to have the things we need. Now I delighted in explaining to her about how our bootstrapping ways—her going without the latest brand-name sneakers; our going on vacation in our own neighborhood instead of on an expensive trip away—Mommy and Daddy working full-time while struggling to build our own small businesses—had allowed Daddy, and now me, to come home and oversee our company with full confidence that our financial needs would be met.

With her fears put to rest, she asked with anticipation, "Does that mean we will all sit down and have dinner together? And will it happen before the sun goes down?" When I said yes, she squeezed my neck in such a way that there was no mistaking how much that mattered to her. I hugged her back because it mattered just as much to me.

Our family operates on an entirely different pace these days. From late May to September, we're working at Akwaaba by the

Sea. We do indeed eat dinner together before the sun goes down, and I love that I wake up in the morning at seven and take a brisk walk on the beach. Later, after we serve our guests breakfast and service their rooms, it's about 1:00 P.M. and the rest of the day is ours to bike ride, relax at the beach, play put-put golf, watch the sunset, or whatever. Okay, so sometimes I make a few work calls as well, and otherwise manage our businesses. But now I also have a standing weekly spa appointment—talk about progress!

Yes, I've traveled far ever since discovering Cape May twelve years ago on a visit at Christmastime. The town's charming Victorian homes, horse-drawn carriages, and soothing afternoon teas have always had a way of chilling me out and helping me to remember to do what we all must do—breathe deeply and fully savor life. That's truly "having what matters."